MEMORIES

Lancashire Cotton Mills

Ron Freethy

COUNTRYSIDE BOOKS
NEWBURY BERKSHIRE

First published 2008
© Ron Freethy 2008
Reprinted 2010

COUNTRYSIDE BOOKS
3 Catherine Road
Newbury, Berkshire

To view our complete range of books,
please visit us at
www.countrysidebooks.co.uk

ISBN 978 1 84674 104 3

*This book is dedicated to Jimmy and Wilfred Jaques,
who were 'Men of Cotton' from the 1870s to the 1960s.*

The cover picture shows weavers at Waterfield Mill in Darwen
celebrating the 1953 coronation.

Designed by Peter Davies, Nautilus Design

Produced through MRM Associates Ltd., Reading
Typeset by CJWT Solutions, St Helens
Printed by Information Press, Oxford

*All material for the manufacture of this book
was sourced from sustainable forests.*

Contents

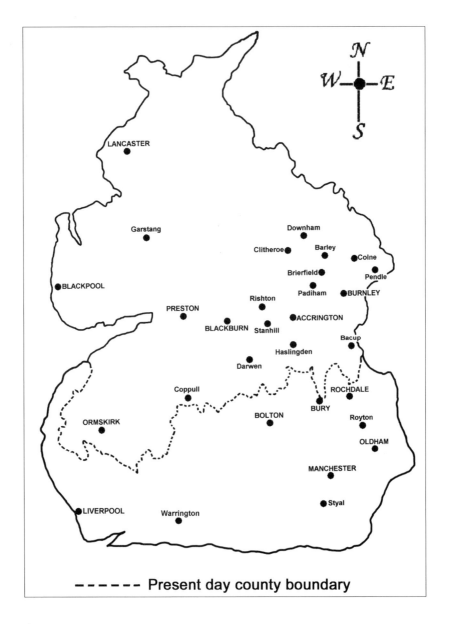

------ Present day county boundary

Foreword

Memories of the Lancashire Cotton Mills highlights the unsung heroes of this era – the ordinary working families of Lancashire. Written in Ron Freethy's inimitable style, his ability to create the feeling of past times is brilliantly portrayed, and throughout, his knack of storytelling is always a delight. His fastidious research and attention to detail uncovers facts not recorded before, and his use of previously unseen photographs completes the picture.

Starting with the growing of cotton, followed by the emergence of handloom weavers, the factory system and the Industrial Revolution, through to boom times and the eventual demise of the industry, the memories of those who worked in the mills are incorporated into each chapter. The book is sprinkled with anecdotes and stories: how in the early days cloth was bleached using sour milk and urine; and the time when mills minted their own coins to pay their workers; the apprentice system at Styal Mill and the 'Wanted' notices used to hunt down runaways; and why Imperial Mill was known as 'The Twelve Apostles'. Lancashire at Play and the Wakes Weeks are covered in detail, when whole towns closed down and families went to Blackpool for the week.

Readers will discover the meanings for 'heirlooms', 'spinsters', and 'popping your clogs', and how the Spinning Jenny got its name. As a descendant of James Hargreaves, the inventor of this machine, this section has a personal and nostalgic relevance for me.

Finally, the 'Last Rites' compares the boom period when Lancashire produced enough cloth before breakfast to supply the UK market – with the remainder of the day's supply going overseas – with the decline of the industry and the period between the First and Second World Wars when around 800 mills were shut down, followed by a similar number closing over the following 50 years.

For historians or just for enjoyment, this is a fascinating book of real interest and value.

Peter Hargreaves,
Hilden Manufacturing Company
and Oswaldtwistle Mills

Acknowledgements

This book attempts to trace the 'rise and fall' of the Lancashire cotton industry. There have been many academic accounts of this process and the present volume is not intended to be another. It is compiled from accounts written or recorded by the men, women and sometimes children who 'worshipped' in the reign of King Cotton. It may come as a surprise that variations on the textile theme were part of Lancashire's contribution to cotton until well into the 1990s.

My thanks are due to more than 500 people who responded to newspaper and local radio requests. Many of these responses have been included in the text and mentioned in this context. Features Editors of local newspapers have been very helpful, especially the *Bury Times*, *Rochdale Observer*, and John Anson and Jill Johnson at the *Lancashire Telegraph*.

Many individuals have also given of their time and expertise and special mention must be made in several instances. Peter Hargreaves, a direct descendant of James Hargreaves, the inventor of the Spinning Jenny, has been a mine of information and has kindly written the foreword to the book. I am grateful as well to Conrad Varley, one-time mill owner and now the manager of the Queen Street Mill Museum in Burnley. Conrad also put me in touch with a group of ex-cotton workers now residing in the Trawden area on the outskirts of Colne.

I must give a very special mention to Keith and Mary Hall, who kept me supplied with tea and information from their weaver's cottage home in the village of Downham. Keith's hobby is collecting postcards and photographs of Lancashire and whilst this work was in its gestation period he searched for and found many of the illustrations included in the book.

My thanks are due to my wife for helpful advice and her word processing skills. The staff of Countryside Books have also played their part with advice and always constructive criticism.

As I put the final full stop to this work, photographs and memories are still coming in by nearly every post. These are being copied and filed so that this proud history of Lancashire Cotton will never be forgotten. Statistics are important, but so are those who remember the decline and fall of King Cotton.

Ron Freethy

Chapter 1

Cotton, Men and Machines

It is often stated that the first cotton to be brought into Britain was via the little port of Sunderland Point near Lancaster in the mid 18th century. This is not true but it is easy to realise why this erroneous statement has so often been repeated. The truth of the matter is that it was the first cotton from the West Indies which was imported through Sunderland Point. Cotton had actually been known in Britain for many years, mostly being brought in from Egypt. But before looking at the history of the industry, the cotton plant itself needs to be described.

The cotton shrub is contained within the genus *Gossypium* and the order *Malvacae*, which includes the Mallow family. There is no way that the British climate could suit cotton and the nearest native relative which we have is the hollyhock.

Scientists have had some difficulty in agreeing on how many species make up the cotton genus, which differ in colour, height and the consistency of the seed but are always bushy plants between three and six feet in height. The flower colour varies from the creamy white of the plant growing on the American uplands and the canary yellow of the Sea Island, to the golden yellow of the Egyptian cotton plant. Perhaps the most attractive variant is the red-seeded Indian cotton and it is easy to see why the local people regarded this plant as sacred as it was so important to their economy.

The cotton 'tree' grows in tropical and sub-tropical regions and only thrives in the area between latitudes 40° North and 30° South. What is certain is that cotton will not grow in areas where there is any frost at all. Neither does cotton thrive where the heat is extreme, and often substantial amounts of water are needed. This can be provided either by natural rainfall or specially engineered irrigation schemes. In some areas of the world today cotton production is causing problems for those demanding ever more and cleaner water.

Experts checking the stapling of cotton at Liverpool Cotton Exchange in the 1940s.

There have been arguments over the centuries with regard to which cotton fibre is the best. Top of most people's list is the Sea Island species called *Gossypium barbadense*. The word *barbadense* means a beard and this certainly has the longest and strongest fibres in the 'boll'. These fibres are actually elongated single plant cells varying in length within the different species from a minimum of 0.75 inches to a maximum of over 2 inches. These lengths are known as the 'staple'. After the flower has withered away, what is known as the 'boll' ripens and eventually bursts to reveal the cotton fibres.

These cotton wool 'balls' or bolls are picked and transported to what have become known as ginneries where they are cleaned to remove dust and infertile seeds before being packed and exported. Initially the 'ginning' in India was done by hand, even though this is labour intensive it hardly mattered in the sub-continent where there was a vast reservoir of workers.

In 1924 the *Textile Manufacturers' Year Book* classified the acceptable staple length of the cotton fibres. These are the Sea Island (1.65 inches), Egyptian (1.50 inches), Pernambuco (1.25 inches), American (1.10 inches) and Indian (0.90 inches). Each spinning mill selected its own preferred staple from huge warehouses which could be visited by customers. In the 1960s I had a great friend called Ivan Cook who told me:

'From the 1930s to the early 1970s I travelled almost every week to Liverpool. My job was to select the best raw cotton to be spun in our mills. Right from the 1790s those who selected the wrong cotton staple soon went bankrupt. We had to select the staple, negotiate a price and arrange to have it delivered. In the early days of the industry the journey to Liverpool was by canal, then there was a rail link from the 1840s but later more road transport was used. I also had to visit the Manchester cotton exchange once each week. Here we negotiated the price of the finished cloth which our mills produced and profit margins could be calculated and export markets negotiated. To avoid confusion, the Liverpool Exchange was open on Mondays and Thursdays whilst the Manchester men operated on Tuesdays and Fridays. Thus imports and exports were nicely balanced. On two occasions I visited America to see how the cotton crop was harvested and although it was more mechanised the marketing negotiations had changed not at all from 1790 to the 1970s when I retired. I had a wonderful job and still worked occasionally as a freelance until 1982.

'I remember the good old days at the Liverpool Exchange in the 1950s when uniformed page boys ran about between customers carrying messages. Those kids were the mobile phones of their day. The Manchester Exchange was even

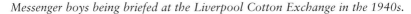

Messenger boys being briefed at the Liverpool Cotton Exchange in the 1940s.

more impressive. When the government from the 1960s decided to 'rationalise' they closed the exchanges but the various staples still had to be sorted out.'

The Manchester Exchange was later converted into an impressive theatre complex.

The History of Cotton

Cotton was grown, spun and woven in India as early as 500 BC, but the Egyptians probably produced it at an even earlier period. One thing accepted by all the experts is that Indian cotton products reached the highest quality and that the art of spinning and weaving spread first to the Near East and then into Europe. The Arabs adapted the Indian techniques and it was they who introduced the processes into Spain by the 8th century. The Arabic name for the textile was 'kutun', from which we derive the name of cotton.

At this time the Moorish towns in southern Spain such as Granada, Seville and Cordova made a goodly living from cotton. By the 13th century the Italian towns were producing high quality cotton and their influence soon spread to the rest of Europe,

Manchester Exchange in 1877 (below) and the same scene in 1964.

especially the Netherlands. Protestant refugees from Holland came to England from the end of the 16th century and into the 17th century. There are records of some Manchester cotton buyers bringing cotton from the Levant and Cyprus in 1640. At that time cotton was referred to as 'vegetable wool'. As the British developed settlements in India, cotton from that country became known as 'calico' whilst that from Mosul in the Middle East became known as 'muslin'. This is why the names are inter-changeable.

In 1793 the American, Eli Whitney, invented the cotton gin which was a machine for separating the fibre from the seed and rubbish (known as dross or trash). This soon meant that America became the world's most important source of the world's raw cotton. The obvious place to land this imported American cotton was at the Atlantic-facing port of Liverpool. This was one of the main factors which allowed Lancashire to become the cotton capital of the world. Although the raw material had to be transported, Lancashire's cotton industry thrived because there was a reliable supply of soft water and efficient machines were invented in this area.

No account of Lancashire's cotton industry would be complete without reference to Egypt. Whilst cotton was produced from ancient times, Egypt did not cultivate the textile commercially until relatively recently. Some exports began in 1821 but it was not until the cotton shortages resulting from the American Civil War of 1860-65 that Egypt had a golden opportunity, especially as its quality was so good.

In the early 1860s the price of cotton rocketed and Egypt greatly increased its area of land under cultivation. After the war, when American supplies were renewed, Egyptian cotton continued to thrive. The Lancashire cotton operatives had learned to respect the quality of the Egyptian crop and continued to order some bolls from this source.

One question is very difficult to answer and that is why did India not grasp the opportunity which Egypt accepted so eagerly? India, the home of cotton, should have dominated the world supply, but perhaps the fact that its staple is the shortest may have restricted its export. The British Cotton Industry did not welcome the inferior short staple which was known as 'Surat'. Thomas Cook of Burnley, who was an expert on cotton supplies, wrote production reports on the problems faced during the American Civil War. He noted that many Burnley mill owners were very religious nonconformists and at a meeting a man prayed for more cotton. 'But not Surat, Lord, not Surat,' called a group of brother operatives!

The American Civil War obviously brought home to the Lancashire men of cotton that it was courting disaster to rely on just one source of supply and they began to survey other parts of the world. They studied not only areas where cotton was already cultivated but also began to develop cotton growing in parts of what was the then expanding British Empire. The Empire Exhibition of 1924 showed that cotton crops were being grown in West, Central and Eastern Equatorial Africa, Rhodesia (Zimbabwe), South Africa, Australia, British Guinea, Cyprus, Mesopotamia (Iraq), Palestine and Fiji. There was, however, a real problem in some of these areas, especially Australia. Cotton picking is very labour intensive and the farmers of Queensland and New South Wales where the climate was suitable did not have enough hands to pick cotton in the quantities demanded by the Lancashire mills.

Growing cotton also had its problems, not least attacks from disease. The boll weevil has caused problems in some, but thankfully not all, regions. Its larvae feed greedily on the cotton boll and are particularly a problem in the United States and the West Indies. Some remedial methods have proved to be successful over the years but the pink boll weevil is still a problem for cotton growers in Egypt.

Two main factors were responsible for Lancashire being crowned King Cotton. Firstly, the strength of the British Navy meant that raw cotton could be safely imported from many regions of the world. Secondly and perhaps more importantly, Britain's Industrial Revolution, the first in the world, was gathering pace. The prominence of engineers and inventors meant that the Men of Cotton and their machines could ensure that production and quality could be guaranteed on a large scale. Industry took the place of home-based production.

The work of these men and their magnificent machines is a vital aspect of textile history and can still be seen to this day, even though cotton fabric production in the county has declined to a mere dribble.

Men and Machines

Lancashire in the mid 1700s was a very different place. The county was largely rural and of little economic importance. The towns were small and the rest of the area very thinly populated. The roads were notoriously poor and the days of turnpikes, canals and railways very much in the future.

The correct method of weaving cotton, and prior to this, wool, had not changed (and still has not changed) for thousands of years. The raw fibres are passed through the processes of cleaning and carding at the beginning and weaving and finishing at the end. As a rule, at that time all these operations were carried on in the workers' homes. The carding, which involved combing the fibres straight, could be done by children. The simple spinning wheel, the property of the women (spinsters), usually stood in the centre of the room. The much bulkier handloom was located in an upstairs room or below in a large cellar and could only be operated by a strong man. This was passed on from the father to his eldest son and here we have the origin of the word 'heirloom'.

Let us now consider these processes in a little more detail before going on to look at Lancashire's contribution to textile machinery, which continued well into the 1980s. The raw cotton had to be converted into yarn. It was first cleaned and then carded. Initially this was done by making use of the dead, dry heads of thistles especially the fruiting heads of the teasel. All these plants grew and still grow plentifully in Britain. (The Latin name for a thistle was *carduus* and here is the origin of the surname, Cardus.)

The teasel heads were eventually replaced by 'hand cards'. These were strips of wood into which were hammered short pieces of wire. Leather was often incorporated into a glove to help the grip. The cards were simple enough in construction and enterprising cottagers could make the tool to fit the hand of the operator. The addition of a handle completed what was a perfect hand tool.

Once the fibres were combed straight they were ready for the spinning process to begin. The spinster turned the spinning wheel with one hand and thus caused the spindle to revolve. With her other hand she drew out the fibres from the cardings, made them into thick threads called rovings and wound these onto her spindle into a lump called a cop. She then varied her operations to spin the rovings into much thinner threads. She also twisted the yarn until it was ready for weaving.

When a hand loom was operated, the yarn was wound into a shuttle. This carried the weft and had to be passed from hand to hand. This obviously restricted the width of the cloth, which seldom exceeded 30 inches. If wider cloth was needed then two weavers were employed with one passing the shuttle to the other.

The weaver could operate his loom much quicker than the spinster could supply him with yarn and it was accepted at the time that six spinsters were required to supply one weaver. By 1725 there were already calls for some form of machinery to be invented. The demand for textiles was becoming greater as people slowly became more affluent and over the next century transportation systems became more efficient.

The great inventions are said by many to have begun in the years between 1733 and 1738 when John Kay of Walmersley, near Bury, realised the need for machines. Art historians, however, will point to the drawing of Leonardo da Vinci (1452-1519) which shows a machine able to produce bobbins of cotton which would wind on the textile evenly. His thoughts thus predated Arkwright by more than two centuries!

John Kay (d.1781): As a child John was apprenticed to a reed maker. Reeds were split and suspended in the frame of the loom and through these passed the warp threads. The child, however, learned a lot from his father who was interested in how his loom worked. When young Kay devised his mechanical shuttle it was originally designed to work wool; it only later became romanticised and is now known as the 'Flying Shuttle'. In essence it was very simple. Two strings were attached to the opposite ends of the lathe or framework of the loom and both were held in the weaver's hand by a peg. By a quick pluck on the wire he could send the shuttle carrying the weft across the loom and it would make its own way between the threads of the warp. This allowed much wider pieces to be woven and of course the weaver could work much faster, thus putting even more pressure on the willing and hard working spinsters.

Kay was not a 'one-off inventor' – his fertile mind was seeking continued modifications to the machinery. He began to replace the reeds by longer-lasting metal rods and he also patented a twisting and carding machine. This, however, put even more stress on the spinsters who were left in the centre of the operations and were asked to work at unattainable speeds.

Not all workers welcomed Kay's improvements and he was the first to suffer from the anger of less enlightened textile operatives who saw a threat to their livelihoods. In 1753 an angry mob wrecked his home and fearing for his safety he fled to France, where he stayed for the rest of his life. It is said that he died a pauper and this would seem to be substantiated because his daughter entered a French convent.

The real problem for Kay was that his patent was easy to copy and although he had the law on his side the fines were minimal. Mary Kay Harvey told me: 'I think my name Kay was an unfortunate coincidence because a relative of mine was a cotton weaver at the time of the Flying Shuttle invention. He joined what was called a Shuttle Club whose members joined together to pay the fines imposed by flouting Kay's patent. It is no wonder the poor chap went bust.'

Kay's son Robert must have remained in England because he invented what became known as the 'drop box' for shuttles in 1760. This made it possible to weave with a succession of wefts of different colours without having to pause in the weaving operations.

At least Kay's name has an honoured place in the annals of the cotton industry and his statue and a garden in the centre of Bury bear witness to his contribution.

The developments to speed up the weaving process meant there was a focus on the need to mechanise carding and spinning. Pioneering work on carding was done by Daniel Bourn of Leominster and John Wyatt of Sutton Coldfield with a working partner, Lewis Paul of Birmingham, who was an acquaintance of Dr Johnson. Both Bourn and Paul took out patents in 1748 showing that they had fixed cards onto rotating cylinders. The idea was good but the practicalities were not really solved. Some producers were, however, prepared to speculate and in 1760 Robert Peel of Stanhill, near Blackburn, tried such a machine. This Peel was the grandfather of the future Prime Minister and it was Peel the elder who began to build up a substantial family fortune.

James Hargreaves (1720-1778): Peel saw the potential of all forms of textile machinery and asked an artisan named James Hargreaves, who lived at nearby Stanhill, to improve on the Wyatt-Paul machine. It is doubtful if even Peel realised that Hargreaves' skill would revolutionise the textile industry.

Here was the end of a cottage industry and the start of the factory system and the Industrial Revolution. At Stanhill, Peel Fold still exists, as does the cottage residence of James Hargreaves. It was here that I met with Peter Hargreaves, a descendant and one who is still involved in the textile industry. Peter spent his time whilst recovering from a life-saving operation by tracing his ancestry and as he told me: 'Long before James, the family had been involved in the woollen trade and I have traced members back to the 15th century when they were known as skilled handloom weavers.'

As a youth Hargreaves was recognised as a skilful weaver but he also had real talent as a carpenter. This is why Peel was aware that here, very close by, was a potential machine maker of great skill.

It is difficult to decide what is fact and what is fiction relating to James Hargreaves. It has been said that he was watching his wife spinning on her wheel whilst he was waiting for her to produce yarn for his loom. She moved and knocked the wheel from a horizontal to an upright position. Both the wheel and the spindle continued to revolve and he then wondered if a number of upright spindles could be set up side by side so that several threads could be spun in one operation. His wife's name was Jenny and so the '*Spinning Jenny*' was developed.

The idea of a sudden flash of inspiration, however, does Hargreaves less than justice because he had been thinking hard about how his carpentry skills could be used to produce carding and spinning machines. It is also relevant to point out that 'jinny' or 'jenny' was a Lancashire slang word for a machine. On the side of Pendle Hill the road linking Roughlee and Newchurch is still called Jinny Lane. No doubt early cotton machines were used in these villages.

A drawing of Hargreaves' Spinning Jenny *in the 1820s.*

Whatever its origins, the Hargreaves contraption worked very well and his 8-spindled machine was eventually increased to 16 and then 32 spindles. In 1770 he took out his patent and eventually 'jinnies' of 120 spindles were being operated from one wheel!

The action of 'drawing' the thread onto the wheel was initially guided by hand, later replaced by a simple but more effective moveable carriage. This had in it a horizontal clasp through which the rovings passed to the spindles. It turned out that the threads could be drawn out and twisted much more evenly than had previously been done by hand.

One would have thought that this brilliant machine would have been welcomed. Alas, as with John Kay there were those who did not welcome progress and were intent upon destroying these 'contrivances of Satan' built by Hargreaves. He laboured on his machines at home and was all too aware of the need for secrecy, but spies with ill intent became suspicious that he was producing lots of superior quality yarn and soon guessed what was afoot. In 1768 they broke into his cottage at Stanhill and smashed his jenny along with any other strange-looking machines. Hargreaves followed Kay's example and fled, not to France but to Nottingham.

He continued to develop his machine along with his more affluent partner, a Mr James, and the pair worked there until Hargreaves' death in 1778. Robert Peel the elder was aware of the Blackburn-based bullies and he relocated his working base to the Rossendale Valley, which he considered at that time to be far enough removed from threat.

Over the years I have had many fascinating conversations with Peter Hargreaves. Peter has kept up the Hargreaves' textile tradition and has perfected his enterprises within a few miles of the Stanhill former home of his illustrious ancestor. He now operates the famous Oswaldtwistle Mills shopping complex from Moscow Mill, which was once one of the most impressive cotton mills in Lancashire. Peter not only told me of his family history but pointed out:

Peter Hargreaves in his 'Time Tunnel'.

'This is why I decided to develop what has become known as the Time Tunnel. This follows a route describing the history of cotton. My study of James Hargreaves has been thorough. He may not have been King Cotton but he was certainly a Prince of Spinners. Our only regret is that unlike other inventors we do not have a portrait of the man himself, but we do have old drawings of his machine. I managed to locate one of these and it is the pride of my collection.'

Visitors to the complex can enjoy a splendid old mill building, do lots of shopping, tour the Time Tunnel and follow the Nature Trail, with a picnic site, which I had the pleasure of designing. Peter continued: 'I love this place when it is full of visitors but I also enjoy chatting to old employees who can remember the days when all the cotton trades were in full swing.' Peter put me in touch with some of these old operatives, whose memories are recorded in the chapters which follow.

Richard Arkwright (1732-1792): Born in Preston and youngest in a family of thirteen, Richard Arkwright was given very little education but he turned out to be both intelligent and ambitious, with a ruthless streak. At the age of thirteen he was apprenticed to a barber in Kirkham and at eighteen he set himself up on his own in Bolton. These premises still exist close to the ancient parish church and opposite the offices of the *Bolton Evening News.* He would shave customers for 1d whilst a haircut was a ha'penny. This undercut the prices charged by rival barbers.

Barbers' shops were traditionally places of gossip and the textile men would have discussed the inventions of men like Kay of Bury and his flying shuttle. It was then that Arkwright became determined to make textile machines and with them his own fortune.

He knew a local clockmaker named Kay (no relation of the flying shuttle inventor) and the pair began to experiment. These projects involved an outlay in capital and Arkwright raised funds by collecting human hair and making it into high quality wigs, which all the gentry sported in those days. He also invented a hair dye and he became a familiar and increasingly affluent figure in and around Bolton.

During his journeys he kept an eye open for rival developments and the early trials of his own machines certainly looked to be promising. The enterprising pair moved to Preston in 1767 and hired a room belonging to the Free Grammar School. This building, now known as Arkwright House, still stands. By 1768 they had a machine functioning well. This involved a system of rollers which revolved at different speeds and drew out the rovings. Hargreaves' spinning jenny could only spin yarn strong enough for the weft, but Arkwright's new and larger machine could spin threads strong enough also to be used in the warp.

This was obviously a major step forward and the new machine also produced a yarn of a more even thickness and a more reliable twist. It was easy to lengthen the rollers and thus make it possible to increase the number of spindles.

Arkwright was also aware of the problems encountered by Kay and Hargreaves, and the parliamentary election of 1768 in Preston increased his worries as political unrest seemed certain. He therefore decided to follow in Hargreaves' footsteps of the year before and took his new invention to Nottingham. There he met a potential partner named Jedediah Strutt, who was a very successful manufacturer of stockings. Working in conjunction with this ambitious company, Arkwright set up his later world-famous cotton spinning mill at Cromford in Derbyshire.

The essential power for this mill came from a reliable spring of soft warm water which emerged from a hillside and close to an old lead mine. The machine henceforth became known as the water frame, but in his 1769 patent Arkwright states that horses were to provide the power. In later years when the power of steam was used the machine became known as the 'throstle', probably because of the singing sound it produced whilst at work. In 1771 Arkwright leased land in Cromford from Peter Nightingale, who was the great uncle of Florence Nightingale.

Arkwright's Water Frame at Helmshore.

Arkwright was never satisfied even though his water frames at Cromford began to make him rich, but never rich enough for his lofty ambitions. He continued to be an inventive genius and improved the carding cylinder. In 1775 he invented a machine for drawing, roving and spinning and he called this machine an 'all in one set'. This Arkwright's till never stopped ringing!

When I spoke to Ian Gibson in the splendid Helmshore Textile Museum he noted:

'We are the only museum in the world that can trace the whole history of these textile machines and visitors come from all parts of the globe to see an original Arkwright water frame which is still capable of working, and a working spinning jenny. We are also an ideal place to understand the contribution of Samuel Crompton and not far away at Bolton is the Hall i' th' Wood Museum which is vitally important in the history of textiles.'

Samuel Crompton (1753-1827): Samuel Crompton was born at Firwood Fold near Bolton where his father had a smallholding. Like many others the family eked out a living by carding, spinning and weaving wool. By the standards of the time, however, the Cromptons were not at all badly off. It is also possible that they had their own sheep, but most likely a much richer middleman delivered the raw fleeces and collected the finished pieces. When Samuel was five the family moved and rented space in the nearby Hall i' th' Wood, a half-timbered building dating back to 1483. It is now a museum, mainly devoted to the life and work of Samuel Crompton. The name is misleading today because gone are the magnificent oak woodlands, which have been replaced by a housing estate and a still operative railway station. Firwood Fold also still exists and is an integral part of a conservation area.

During the year of the move to Hall i' th' Wood, Crompton's father died and his mother became even more devoted to her only son. She encouraged him to read and write but at fourteen he was also a skilled operator of one of Hargreaves' spinning jennies. By sixteen he was an accomplished weaver but he was ever eager for knowledge and studied algebra and trigonometry at evening school in Bolton. Like his father, he was an accomplished artisan and treasured the tools his father bequeathed him and which were meant to be used in the construction of an organ. These tools were used instead to construct a machine first called the Hall-i'-th'-Wood wheel.

In 1774 when Crompton was 21 he regarded himself as a weaver, not a spinner, and was frustrated by the poor quality yarn which he had to work with and which was always breaking. He decided to invent a machine to produce high quality yarn. This was not easy because he only had his father's organ tools to work with. He needed money and he augmented his income by making a violin and playing this in the orchestra of a Bolton Theatre. Even more vital was to keep the development of his machine away from the envious eyes of potential engine breakers. He often worked through the night and after five years he had made good progress. As he was getting ready to test his machine the spinners and weavers of

Blackburn began to engage in angry confrontations, which involved smashing any machine which operated more than 20 spindles.

Crompton the inventor put his talents to work by constructing a trap door leading up to the rafters. He floored this space, dismantled his machine and re-assembled it in the roof. In 1779 the machine was complete and it combined the basic principles of Hargreaves' spinning jenny and Arkwright's roller wheels. The machine had a moveable carriage, on which a number of spindles were erected, and in addition there were two rollers and through these the carded slivers were drawn. The original design was to have the motive force provided by hand but by 1770 Crompton had adapted his machine to be operated by water. It was probably around this time that the term 'mule' was used as it was a combination of Hargreaves' and Arkwright's machines.

Whilst Crompton obviously copied the principles of the other two machines, he introduced the concept of a moving carriage, a device which meant that very large machines could be constructed. Crompton more than any other inventor provided the impetus for mass production and literally sowed the most important seed in the early history of the cotton industry.

The sad thing is that while Arkwright was a tough businessman who made money, Crompton failed to compete on both these counts. This is strange in view of the fact that Crompton was by far the more intelligent of the two. Yet he was short of both money and business acumen and he did not even have enough resources to patent his own machine. All he did was to spin a much improved yarn on his machine, which he had to operate in secret.

In retrospect it is obvious that Crompton's yarn was of such quality and quantity that he could not long keep his secret! He was soon besieged by interested visitors, not all being honest or friendly. Some actually brought ladders in order to see into the upstairs rooms and one is said to have bored an observation hole in the roof through which they could look down!

It soon became obvious, even to Crompton, that his secret was out and he had to accept the promises of local manufacturers.

These men did not honour their obvious obligations and Samuel Crompton became embittered for the rest of his life in consequence.

It has to be accepted that Crompton not only had no business acumen but also that he was profoundly unlucky. He petitioned Parliament for a grant and in May 1812 his wish was granted. Spencer Perceval's government had agreed to provide Crompton with the then large sum of £20,000. On 11 May 1812 Perceval was assassinated and in consequence Parliament was dissolved. This also killed the financial hopes of Crompton because the new Prime Minister was not so enthusiastic as had been the ill-fated Perceval. Eventually Parliament did provide him with £5,000 but it seems that he then made investments which were not successful.

Without the inventor's knowledge some friends built up subscriptions which provided him with an annuity of £63, but he was still a very bitter man until his death in 1827. It was a further 30 years before his native Bolton saw fit to celebrate his work by creating an impressive bronze statue. These days all the textile world knows the name of Crompton and the Hall i' th' Wood Museum is a fitting memorial to a great inventor.

Jim Brodie, who is still working as Bury's lighting engineer and is now into his seventies, served his time as a textile engineer and pointed out why the mule and its continued improvements have stood the test of time.

'I began as an apprentice for the Casablanca High Draft Company in 1954 and was involved in adapting ring frame spinning machines for the needs of engineering companies including Platt Brothers of Oldham, Dobson and Barlows of Bolton, Tweedale and Smalley of Rochdale and Howard and Bullough, who had their huge Globe Works in Accrington. Most people think that these comparatively new ring frames were an improvement on the old mules. They were not, but they did have advantages – they were much faster, did not have huge moving parts and were therefore lighter and occupied less space, and did not require so much maintenance. What the ring spinners did was to produce cotton thread much quicker. We all knew, however, that these machines produced a much coarser thread than the mules. Places like Rochdale and Oldham quickly went on to ring spinning because they were catering for a mass market. On the other hand Bolton was famous for producing high quality fine thread, which was no doubt a throw back from the Crompton days. Bolton and District therefore kept their mules. I think that spinning machines changed more than the weaving tackle, but even there the loom still showed that inventors did not rest on the laurels of Cartwright.'

Dr Edmund Cartwright (1743-1822):
For many centuries the production of textiles was a labour intensive process and weaving on a heavy loom required not only skill but also physical strength and stamina. This, as we have seen, was a male dominated cottage industry and one which was jealously protected. Any mech-anically operated loom was therefore feared. In the light of future developments, Cartwright's pioneering work on the production of a power loom seems not only sensible but inevitable. In the late 18th century however, such a development was fraught with physical and personal danger. It is unusual in the sense that the inventor of the power loom was an academic and not an artisan.

Dr Edmund Cartwright, a fellow of Magdalene College in Oxford, was visiting Matlock in 1784. He met and spoke with fellow travellers who happened to be merchants from Manchester. From them he heard of the need for a mechanically-driven loom, which would keep pace with the spinning frames of Arkwright and Crompton. It is said that these conversations inspired him to visit Arkwright's mill at nearby Cromford.

All this set Cartwright's fertile brain working and in 1785 he took out a patent for the first 'power loom'. The history of this invention is as much a part of the history of the Yorkshire woollen industry as that of the rival county of Lancashire which devoted itself almost entirely to cotton.

Cartwright's first power loom was, to say the least, very crude – it was constructed of wood and was powered by a bull. He worked constantly on improvements and by 1789 he had set up a factory in Doncaster. In 1791 a Manchester firm purchased 400 power looms and Radcliffe, Horrocks, Roberts and Johnson improved the loom. By 1815 the power loom was in use throughout most of Lancashire. By this time the work of the inventors mentioned above had ensured the advent of the Industrial Revolution in what became the Cotton County.

As I spoke to cotton operatives who had laboured all their lives in the industry, they left me in no doubt that inventions did not cease with the great men of history. Arthur English, who still lives in Trawden, near Colne, told me:

'All my ancestors worked in cotton and my mother had me in a cradle while she was weaving. I became a weaver but I went to night school in Nelson and learned about loom making. At night school we studied the lives of the early men of cotton but we also had modern day heroes and right up until the 1960s clever men were fine-tuning and improving the workings of all types of machinery. We knew of the work of William Thompson of

Arthur English – a man with cotton in his soul.

Clitheroe, who in 1899 produced a machine at the Whipp Brothers Mill which supplied oil to the machinery without the need to stop the piece working. This saved lots of time and money. I knew too of Whites of Colne who were making improvements to cotton machines until well into the 1960s.'

These memories were echoed by Barrie Whittaker of Burnley, who wrote:

'I served my time as a fitter, first at Pemberton's Waterloo Foundry, who were textile engineers and loom makers. I then went on to Pilling and Sons of Colne doing the same job. This was in the early 1950s. In 1966 I was appointed as Maintenance Engineer at Robert Pickles and Sons, at their Cairo Mill in the Whittlefield area of Burnley. I was there for more than seven years and I must admit that these

White and Sons were one company making improvements to cotton machinery.

were the best years of my working life. We did all sorts of work from the maintaining and repairing of looms to servicing and adapting ancillary machinery including the steam engines working in the textile trade. These skills were different to those found in any other industry and the folks I worked with were great. My boss was one of the best engineers that I have ever met and he would sit down and invent techniques to make the machines work better. I still treasure my photographs of the main steam engine at Cairo Mill which I had to strip down and make new parts for to keep it running. I also still have some of the working drawings I used when working at Pillings. I've enjoyed writing these notes in spite of my arthritis because the work we loved doing does need to be remembered.'

I once worked with Frank Carson, who laughs at his name which he shares with a comedian. Frank finished his working life as a laboratory technician. He still lives in Burnley and recalls:

The famous Pilling-designed loom.

'I served my time as a carpenter in the cotton industry, my job was to look at drawings of machinery and produce a wooden pattern. This was then pressed into a sand mould into which molten metal was poured. It was then filed and fine-tuned to fit. People think that invention stopped with the old timers but actually it went on right to the bitter end.'

Research into cotton fabrics and machines continued all through the Lancashire textile history and one of the leading authorities was the Shirley Institute. Based in Didsbury near Manchester, it was funded by donations from mill owners who always ensured that they got value for money. Here existing machines were adapted and new techniques devised to replace labour intensive jobs by machines which worked fast and did not get tired or break down. The work of these 'Bobbin Boffins' has never been fully appreciated, as Colin Webb of Burnley told me:

'I learned my textile trade at night school at Burnley Tech and we had regular contact with work done at the Shirley Institute. Their deliberations were eagerly read and treated like words in the Bible.'

During the 1960s and 1970s I visited the Textile Department at the Burnley and Nelson Technical College and spoke at length to the men of cotton who lectured there. It was then that I appreciated that some firms specialised in producing fabrics to serve different functions. They therefore needed to adapt their machines to suit the required product.

One such company was Grenfell, who became world famous for the manufacture of cold weather clothing and tents. Many explorations to the North and South Pole and to mountains like the Alps and the Himalayas used Grenfell fabric. Trading began at Meadow Bank Mill in Brierfield in 1908 and just after the First World War moved to Lodge Mill in Burnley. The cloth had to be wind and water proof and yet had to 'breathe' to prevent the wearer from perspiring. Only Egyptian cotton was found to be suitable and the looms had to be strengthened to cope with the heavy finished cloth. Even then other problems had to be solved. The fabric was so waterproof that it was all but impossible to get the dye into it. The problems were all solved, however, and by the 1930s no Everest expedition went to do battle with the elements without Grenfell tents and clothing.

The final words concerning Men of Cotton are those of Eric Goddan, who lives in Brierfield and who worked as a tackler all his life until his retirement in the 1980s. He told me:

'Anybody who thinks that looms never developed over the years should think again. We had regular visits from loom makers pointing out improvements they had made and also how other looms could be modified to work more efficiently. Then came the Jacquards, which were additions to the normal loom. These were bolted on to the loom and were like a high frame above the machine. They were like early computers and meant that patterns of different colours could be woven into the cloth. It was a wonderful invention and we had to learn to service them. This meant carrying a ladder and using this to climb up on top and fettle it if owt went wrong. There were funny instances when practical jokers pinched your ladder and left you stranded. There were also more serious events when careless tacklers fell off the frame. There were no soft landings onto a solid Lancashire loom even if it was not actually working.'

Obviously the development of new machines and especially the improvements to old designs created a knock-on effect on the people who operated them. This aspect of family life is the subject of the next chapter.

Chapter 2

Factories and Families

The history of cotton was from its earliest days very much a family affair. The textile industry in Lancashire began in cottages with the children doing the carding, the women the spinning and the men the weaving. As mills replaced cottages there was still employment for men, women and children, but in a much less healthy environment.

The first change from family to factory came when machines developed, which were first operated by human or animal muscle and later by water. Lancashire was ideally suited for using powered machines because of its hilly nature and high rainfall. Even small streams tumbling down to the larger but more sluggish rivers could operate small waterwheels which could turn a number of machines for both spinning and weaving. Where a watercourse moved too slowly an artificial waterfall called a weir was constructed.

Before the days of steam, and the huge grimy mill towns associated with it, came the cotton village situated close to a watercourse. There are many such villages in cotton country

An old watermill photographed in the 1870s.

which can be explored and provide excellent walking trips, full of industrial archaeology and unspoiled countryside.

Just off the A6 near Garstang the river Brock and its even smaller tributaries can be explored by following the signs towards Beacon Fell. The Brock Valley Nature Walk starts from a pleasant car park and picnic site close to Brock Bridge. During the 18th century the fast flowing river was a focal point for the industrialisation of textiles. At the height of its working life the area had four watermills sited on the stream, which is a tributary of the Wyre which reaches the sea at Fleetwood.

Initially there was one paper mill but this was demolished around 1790 and replaced by a cotton mill. This had sixteen spinning frames and back-up personnel such as joiners and blacksmiths, and cottages for the workers plus stables for horses which carried the finished cloth to market and brought in raw materials.

I have enjoyed many enjoyable conversations with the eminent textile historian Chris Aspin, who has explored these old mill sites for more than 30 years. He told me that in the Brock Valley,

'All these buildings have now collapsed and are almost swallowed up by vegetation but the ruins can still be located. There are also damp areas which were once the mill ponds, as a failed attempt was later made to convert to steam in order to compete with the complex of mills in the expanding towns. Some reminders of the gardens cultivated by the mill workers can still be seen and there are apples and pear trees plus raspberry bushes which once provided vital food. No doubt each family kept a pig in the garden and was also sure of extra but essential income from the little mill. People were much healthier working in these early water-powered mills than those who came later, who were forced to migrate into hovels in towns full of steam, soot and smoke!'

Within easy walking distance of Bolton is the historic village of Barrow Bridge, once surrounded by magnificent upland countryside. During the 1960s, whilst teaching at the nearby Smithills Grammar School, I researched the early history of cotton in Bolton. What was eventually the cotton spinning town was once called Bolton-in-the-Moors and developed from a small village to a huge town. At this time cotton was replacing wool and inventors such as the local lad Samuel Crompton had helped to change the profile of industry from village cottages to town mills.

The intermediate period between hamlet and town is clearly seen at Barrow Bridge, which is a time-encapsulated reminder of the early days of the Industrial Revolution.

There had been a small textile mill on this site for some time when, in 1830, the complex was bought by Robert Gardner of Manchester. He appointed a very able mill manager called Thomas Bailey and the partnership worked so well that profits soared and new mills were constructed. This was the blueprint for many developments which soon followed elsewhere in the county.

This progressive pair looked after their workforce and provided them with pleasant houses, each being given its own garden. By comparison with later town developments these conditions were sheer luxury. The children had a splendid school and for the adults there was a lecture hall and a college institute.

The Barrow Bridge mill complex, seen at the height of its prosperity about 1900, was an example of how to accommodate a workforce.

In 1851 Prince Albert and Benjamin Disraeli visited Barrow Bridge, which was then regarded as the model of its age. Disraeli was not only a politician and Prime Minister but also a successful novelist who reflected the social history of the times. His novel *Sybil*, published in 1845, described the life of workers during this period. The transition from cottage to mill is also graphically portrayed in Robert Neil's *The Mills of Colne* which was published in 1951. At Barrow Bridge the two six-storey mills were demolished in 1913 but the rest of the settlement remains as a monument to a bygone age when cotton production was a more humane enterprise than it became very soon afterwards.

There are many other settlements in Lancashire which reflect the history of early cotton production based upon water power. At Barrowford is the Pendle Heritage Centre and from its shop it is possible to obtain a leaflet called the *Water Power Trail*. Whilst following this there are to be seen restored mills powered by water, old handloom weavers' houses, early spinning factories and Pendle Water, which once provided the essential power.

Nearer to Pendle are the villages of Roughlee and Barley which provide other reminders of the early days of the Industrial Revolution. At Roughlee the mill building itself has gone but the 'waterfall' near the school is actually a weir and the mill lodge dug to provide water for the engine is now a trout fishery.

Near the car park at Barley is the tiny hamlet of Narrowgates, set on the banks of Pendle Water. Here William Hartley's cotton twisting mill has now been converted into a private residence but is still dominated by its huge chimney, built when water power gave way to steam. The old mill workers' cottages have also been successfully converted.

Above the village are Barley Green's two cotton mills which were also constructed in the early 1800s. In 1862 as many as 200 looms were busy clattering away. Floods damaged the mills so badly that year that they never recovered, but another disadvantage was that they were too far away from roads, rail and canal to compete economically.

Another fascinating hamlet close to Colne is Wycoller, which for years was referred to as the 'hidden village' but which is now the focus of an excellent country park. In the days when the Brontë sisters walked from Haworth, Wycoller was a handloom weavers' stronghold and the history is now explained in a museum based in an old barn. There is evidence to prove that Charlotte Brontë based her 'Ferndean Manor' on Wycoller Hall. One of the Brontës' relatives was called Eyre and we therefore also have the origins of the title of the famous novel.

On the opposite side of Pendle Hill is the charmingly unspoiled village of Downham, filmed as the setting for the TV series *Born and Bred*. One of the cottages used as the village shop in the series is lived in by Keith and Mary Hall. Mary told me: 'Our village cottages were once the homes of handloom weavers but they worked with wool. We are proud of our early textile industry and when you sit in our parlour and look at the ceiling beams you can see the design of the handloom dwellings. In some of the cottages you can see a trapdoor in the upper storey. Bales of wool could be lifted into the loft and the heavy woven piece taken out onto a waiting cart.'

Mary Hall's enjoyment of living in the hub of history is echoed by Mrs Joan Proctor, who lives in Stable Cottage in the Sheer Brow area of Blackburn:

> 'I love my old handloom weaver's cottage which is close to the centre of Blackburn but Sheer Brow was once a self-contained hamlet, now swallowed up by old mills and the streets associated with them. My cottage still has the delivery yard and later this was used as a fishmonger's shop with the appropriate notice still on the wall.'

When I was old enough to enjoy my first pint, in the early 1950s, I drank in the Engine Inn at Cark, now in Cumbria and close to the station. Later I found out that the 'Engine' referred to was not a locomotive but the power plant of the Cark cotton mill which was destroyed by fire in 1935. In the 1970s I found a small

Cark Mill in 1890 (above) and after the fire in May 1935.

number of coins which were marked with the name of the mill. These were produced during the time when the wages paid to workers put a strain on the Mint and not enough small coins were available. Many mills made their own coins which local shops took in payment and were later exchanged as more official coins became available. These coins are found more and more often as metal detector enthusiasts locate them.

At Chipping near Preston there is now a thriving chair factory which was built in 1785 as Kirk Mill and is a fine example of a largely unaltered mill building of the period. Although obviously not now working, the water wheel is still in situ.

Also worth exploring is the Cheesden Brook, which runs beneath the road from Edenfield to Rochdale. This now deserted valley once had fifteen mills powered by the brook in its six-mile descent towards Bury and its confluence with the Irwell. I once spent a happy day with Brian Ashworth tracing the sites of the old watermills which he has located along the Cheesden Valley:

'Folk hereabouts love the fact that we have an area which shows how in the early days of cotton, water was the main source of power and over the last 20 years I have mapped out these factories which literally were watermills. This aspect of Lancashire's history needs to be recorded and celebrated. I have spoken to several people whose ancestors worked in those mills in the old days. Their families have memories of their great-grandparents who made their living first from handloom weaving and farming and then in these early cotton mills.'

As already briefly mentioned, textile production can be divided into three processes: namely spinning, weaving and finishing which included dyeing and printing. During the Industrial Revolution each process evolved its own design of building and involved a variety of skilled operatives.

Spinning

As spinning mill architecture evolved, five storeys became the norm but later six floors seem to have been regarded as the most economic. There is some truth in the suggestion that potential manufacturers consulted a small nucleus of architects and each had what amounted to a pattern book. Peter Hargreaves told me, 'In my library of cotton books I have *The Fine Cotton Spinnings Association* publication which was a privately printed volume published in 1909 and which was really a pattern book from which the owners of spinning mills could choose their preferred mill.'

The mill was then built and furnished with the correct number of machines to fit this formula. It is no wonder that the mill towns specialising in spinning such as Oldham, Rochdale and Bolton grew very quickly and looked so similar. When seen at night, the overall appearance of a typical spinning mill with its large number

Purpose-built, multi-storey spinning mills. Swainston and Birley's Mills in Preston, seen here in 1834, worked more hours than most during the Cotton Famine of the early 1860s.

of small windows superficially resembled a modern day cruise ship. The owners felt that small windows should be used in order to retain more humidity and also to conserve heat and thus use less fuel. Many chose 'frosted' glass so that workers did not waste time by looking out at the scenery.

Mill owners were keen on profits but they were also proud of their buildings, to such an extent that impressive names were given to them. Here we have India Mill in Darwen, Mavis Mill at Coppull (named after a family member) and the Bee Mill at Royton where the owner hoped his workers' efforts would resemble those of busy bees!

In the early cottage industries the spinners were women but in the huge mills the spinners were almost all men. They worked barefoot on wooden floors and in temperatures varying between 75°F and 98°F. The finer the thread to be spun, the higher the temperature had to be, because the higher the temperature the softer the cotton fibres were and the easier they were to work.

The early prosperity of cotton spinning was initially due to Crompton's Mule. In retrospect it is accepted that although the mule did provide a very even yarn it was also large and clumsy in operation. The usual width of a cotton spinning floor was about 100 ft but this was fully occupied by the carriage, which was mounted on wheels and twisted the yarn as it moved and then was wound onto a cop before returning to the start of the process. This was, to say the least, noisy, as I discovered on a visit to the Helmshore Mills Textile Museum where one floor is full of old but still very functional spinning machines.

In contrast ring spinning, which was invented in the 1890s, took up much less space, but the Lancashire cotton men were always slow – most would say too slow – to accept change. Even in the 1920s when ring spinning machines were said to be much more efficient, the Lancashire men were reluctant to spend money on new machines when times were hard and so their operatives kept the often obsolete mules going. However, as noted in the last chapter, there were some good reasons for keeping the mules running. The quality of yarn produced by mules was initially

Primrose Mill and Lodge, Clitheroe

A view of the Primrose cotton mill, Clitheroe

43

superior to that coming from the ring mills. With ring frames, existing buildings could increase their capacity but installing new (often imported) machinery was one step too far for most men in search of short-term profits.

Ring spinning was also much less of a health hazard than operating mules. Another problem was that when short or medium staple cotton was being processed in the card room the air became filled with what was called 'fly'. This was almost as fine as dust and when inhaled led to cancerous growths. It is no accident that the now world famous Christie Hospital originated in Manchester in order to study and treat the diseases of cotton workers. Mule spinners were also adversely affected by coming in contact with the oil with which the machines were lubricated. The region around the groin seems to have been particularly vulnerable.

In contrast, ring spinning demanded dexterity and discipline and as a consequence increasing numbers of young females were needed by the few far-sighted mill owners who grasped the value of investment.

The whole of the cotton industry became ever more competitive. Unexpected contenders were the Swiss, who first imported cotton machines from Lancashire before adapting these to produce their own designs. By the early 1930s it became obvious that an economic slump was on the way and that Lancashire would probably suffer more than most. Cotton was in decline but its eventual death was slow, and not at all pleasant, as will be described in some of the following chapters.

Weaving

The design of a weaving shed was very different from that of a spinning mill, but here too there were designers who would erect made-to-measure and highly functional buildings. A weaving shed was almost always single-storey and had solid stone floors. This is because the machinery was heavy and even more noisy. There were saw-shaped roof windows which allowed the many weavers enough light to see their clattering looms. Workers who knew both types of mill referred to the 'song' of a spinning mill and the

*A typical weaving mill, now demolished, at Ribchester in the Ribble valley.
Look at the single-storey sheds and the angled windows to admit
maximum light.*

'clattering ear splitting noise' of a weaving mill, which had its own
inherent dangers. The looms were powered by moving driving
belts, pulleys and overhead shafts. Careless workers could be
killed by these contraptions and it is easy to see why mill girls tied
their hair back tightly using headscarves.

When I spoke at some length to Pat Whiteley in June 2007 she
pointed out another hazard:

> 'Your hair was a problem but the only bad injury I had
> was when a rogue spindle flew out of a loom at very high
> speed and buried itself in my back. It meant a day or two
> in hospital and it took me time to recover because it
> affected my shoulder. The spindles were more than 1 ft
> long. I knew of some weavers who had loose spindles
> strike their eyes so I suppose I was lucky. I was also lucky

that the mill owner paid me whilst I was off work, but perhaps he was lucky because in the situation today accidents like mine would result in high levels of compensation.'

The mill girls had a specific uniform including headgear which kept the rain out on the way to the mill. This could then be used to tie back their hair to keep it out of the way of dangerous machinery.

The weaving shed was not heated because it was thought that the machinery itself generated enough heat. This may have been true except in the early morning in winter when the iron-constructed Lancashire looms would literally have been painful to the touch.

This was an insignificant health hazard compared with the introduction of gas lighting, with the only advantage to the workers being the light which it provided. To the mill owners the gas enabled profits to soar because the mills could more easily be operated on a shift system. There was often a gas light provided over each loom and because the gas was generated from a single point there was linking piping everywhere. Gas leakages were always a problem and an overlooker toured the mill carrying a taper and a supply of mantles. The atmosphere was always heavy with gas fumes and each and every worker left a shift with a severe headache.

Pat Whiteley knows of the dangers when working in a weaving shed. She always wore her hair short.

Eighty-six-year old Rita Ratcliffe of Haslingden remembers,

'Even at the start of the war [1939] our mill was still lit by gas. We worked Saturday mornings and our tackler's job was to turn on the gas and then walk down the alleys and light the mantles. On this particular morning he missed lighting some of the mantles and by ten o'clock I had developed a headache and was sick and dizzy. We were lucky that there was no explosion but it took six of us a day or two to recover but we had still to work through it. Idle hands made up no wage packets.'

The presence of gas also brought with it the threat of fire in weaving mills. This, however, was a minor risk compared with the dangers of fire associated with spinning mills. Here there were wooden floors impregnated with oil and a five- or six-storey mill could be destroyed in a matter of minutes. All mill workers became proficient in putting out fires because it took time for fire brigades to arrive with their inefficient pumping equipment, often travelling several miles to reach the scene by horse and cart!

Some fires have gone down in the annals of the cotton industry, including the fate of the Ellenroad Spinning Mill at Milnrow on the outskirts of Rochdale. The five-storey spinning mill was built in 1892, with water for its massive boilers extracted from the river Beal. The mill was very profitable until 19 January 1916. At that time the huge engine was powering 99,756 mule spindles constructed by Platts of Oldham. At half past two in the afternoon George Taylor, who was a mule operator, noticed a spreading fire. The mill was evacuated whilst specially trained workers tried to control the fire. It took a horse-drawn fire brigade from Oldham until 4.30 pm to arrive. By 5.30 pm the fire was contained but then a wind blew up and fanned the hot embers which spread to other areas and within minutes the rest of the Ellenroad Mill was an inferno. All that remained was the fire-damaged engine house with its two huge engines called Victoria and Alexandra.

Until as late as the 1950s the insurance payout for this mill was the largest in the history of the cotton industry. In 1919, after the First World War, the decision was made to rebuild the mill and follow the pattern of the old structure. The company sensibly made the decision not to replace the mules but to install brand new ring spinning machines. This meant modifying the two engines but the problem was that the original engineers had gone out of business. The Clayton Goodfellow Company of Blackburn successfully modified the engines and the horse power of the boilers of Victoria and Alexandra was increased from 1,850 to 2,850. This was then the most powerful spinning unit in the world!

Some cotton spinners not long retired can remember working on mules and ring spinning machines. Wilf Reynolds, who still lives in Rochdale, has memories spanning three generations:

'I worked on a very modern ring spinning machine until I retired in 1979. My grandfather had been a spinner all his life but he first worked on a huge mule machine which Arkwright would have recognised. He taught me about the history of the machines and I knew about the Kay flying shuttle which was largely humanly operated and the mules which were powered by steam engines and had hundreds of spindles producing thread. By the 1960s the machinery was moved by powerful jets of water, later by compressed air and powered by electricity. These modern techniques, providing they were serviced properly, were much quicker to operate and even more importantly there were far fewer accidents. My grandad and his mates all had industrial injuries and other health problems associated with the working of cotton. As a young lad I knew that the mill was not a healthy spot but by the 1960s things were much better. These improvements came just as the industry was dying a death. As my grandad would have said, "This were a great shame".'

Wilf mentioned to me in 2005 that Ellenroad was once regarded as the best mill of its type in the area. The Ellenroad Spinning Mill remained profitable but in 1970 steam was forced to give way to electric power. The huge boilers and engines were silenced. In 1982 the mill closed and the building was demolished with the notable exception of the boiler house and engines. These and the 220-ft high chimney are now looked after by the Ellenroad Steam Museum Society. This admirable society has restored the boiler house and Victoria and Alexandra hum, steam and hiss away on the first Sunday of every month except January. There are regular exhibitions relating to the history of textiles and there is a bookshop and café.

The boilers and the twin engines are impressive but no less awe-inspiring is the huge flywheel driven by these engines. On its diameter of more than 30 ft there are 44 grooves. When the mill was functioning fully, ropes were wound onto the grooves and these were attached to leather belts which drove the machinery.

Ellenroad steam engine.

This led to lots of work for those who made ropes and belts. Even today with no machinery to drive, the rotating flywheel still creates a fearsome draft of warm air. The flywheel revolves at 58.5 revolutions per minute and weighs 80 tonnes, which is about the same as nine double decker buses!

The understanding of the power of this machinery is vital to those interested in the history of cotton mills. Without the power plant not one person could work and a good chief engineer was a very important person respected by bosses and workers alike. Engineers worshipped their engines and this is why so many are named after ladies!

The Lancashire boiler could always be relied upon to produce predictable steam and plenty of smoke. A careless engineer could be the direct cause of loss of life or putting operatives out of work. When work ended on Saturday afternoon the engineer had to supervise the damping down of the boilers and release the excess steam. He also had to ensure that the boilers did not run out of water. A Blackburn engineer made these errors in the early 1920s and a violent explosion blew the boiler covers through the roof with such force that they were never seen again. In the late 1940s Marlene Jaques knew of an engine flywheel becoming detached from its mountings in a mill on Rylands Street in Burnley and smashing through a wall.

I spoke at length to Eric Goddan who is now retired and living in Brierfield and who remembers this Rylands Street event very clearly:

'It all began in the engine room when an oiler had a rag hanging out of his back pocket. This got caught up in the engine governor and the belting on the machines therefore went faster. The girls turned off their looms because of the speed and when these were off the wheel went even faster. This then broke out of its mounting and careered through the shop floor and through the wall. Weavers were trapped under the wrecked looms and it is a miracle that nobody was seriously injured. Some of the old timers still talk of this but few of 'em know just what happened.'

This glorious mill was devastated by fire in 1916

The hazards of explosion and fire have become part of the folk memory of each of the mill towns. The reason is not too far to seek because either of these events meant an extra danger for the workers. A mill not working was a real worry for those who knew the horrors of the pawn shop and the shame and fear of entering the workhouse. What all workers wanted was to see smoke pouring from mill chimneys, the sounds of the factory whistle summoning the people to work and of their clogs on the cobbled streets as they hurried to the mill gates.

In the early days mill chimneys were known as 'smoke-pokes' and what an accurate descriptive term this was. The earliest chimneys were square in section and not very high. These are generally found in the early mills as steam was replacing water power. The low square chimneys can still be seen at Barley and Spen Brook close to Nelson whilst the Ellenroad structure (opposite) is of circular construction. Why should this be?

Fire at Lodge Mill (also known as Byerden Mill), Burnley, in October 1905. Many a football team would have been glad of such a gate to see them, but the people watching knew that hardship was on the way as they lost jobs and wages.

Soon the use of bricks and better design plus larger engines and more smoke meant increases in the height of chimneys in an effort to take atmospheric pollution higher and away from the town centres. Circular chimneys meant less resistance to wind and so heights of over 200 ft could be built with safety. The 220-ft high chimney at Ellenroad is a fine example and has been mentioned above.

In my early days of working in television I had several conversations with the late Fred Dibnah, the famous steeplejack and engineering enthusiast, and I interviewed him as he was felling a chimney:

'I'm sorry to see these owd chimleys being dropped. In the early days chimleys were square in shape and were too easily affected by the wind so they decided to make 'em round. They also med a platform towards the top which were good for us 'Jacks'. They were mostly of brick and so we had a lot of pointing to do. Folk often think that steeplejacks were mad and I suppose we were but we took notice of all safety rules such as they were in them days. When steeplejacks get together which is 'norallthar ofen' they have tales to tell. In my day I were busy knocking down chimleys but the old timers were hard at work repairin' 'em. One old lad told me of working on a chimley at a Belmont dye works and a bird of prey kept flyin' round him as this were its nestin' site. It were a real aggressive bugger and he had to keep an eye open fer it.'

Some mill owners wished to break records and in 1870 the India Mill chimney in Darwen rose to a height of 300 ft. The owner stipulated that the chimney had to be specially strengthened because he wanted it to be square in section. It was built of local brick to resemble the campanile (bell tower) of St Mark's Square in Venice.

The function of a high chimney was not just to ensure that the soot from the smoke did not all fall in the centre of production. It

The chimney at Belmont Dyeworks being repaired in the 1960s.

was also essential to provide the draught needed in order for the ever larger coal-fired boilers to work efficiently. To the mill owners it was this, rather than the threat of pollution, which was important.

Despite the height of the chimneys the atmosphere around the mill towns was so acidic that old buildings – and even statues to the men of cotton – were damaged by the pollution. As Fred Dibnah mentioned to me, the mortar between the bricks eroded and regular repointing was essential.

The cleaning of chimneys was not the only dirty job associated with steam power as Danny Bellshaw, who now lives and works in Roughlee but was associated with the cotton industry for many years, recalled:

'I always preferred the open air life and worked on farms but we were not well paid and I got a job which were called 'wheeling out'. This was weekend work and when the mills shut down on Saturday morning the boiler fires were damped down and cleaned. When it cooled down by Sunday two tough lads crawled inside the boiler – Walter and Harold they was called – and they scraped out the pipes. They scraped the ash behind them and I had to shovel it up and put it in a wheelbarrow which I then had to dump. All three of us had to work hard so that the boilers could be fired up ready for Monday morning. Later I became a weaver and worked weekends on the farm. We didn't have a holiday because our Wakes weeks coincided with hay time. I knew one boiler man who was a good singer and often gave his rude rendition which he called "Keep the work fires burning".'

The bleaching and finishing of the cotton, whilst not so labour intensive, was responsible for a great deal of river and canal pollution, and these are gradually but impressively improving following the closure of many works.

My working life involved dealing with water pollution and in the early 1980s I was sent to a river which was said to be the cleanest in Lancashire. No wonder it looked clean because it was set alongside a bleach works. Even the gravel of the river bed was white, but the bleach leaking out from the works had over the years killed all forms of wildlife including the plants. Thus, Lancashire's cleanest river – a tributary of the Irwell – was in fact a liquid chemical bleach works! Once this was dealt with the river improved, later the plant closed and the river now supports trout in some numbers.

At first the bleaching of cloth was a long drawn out process but the basic principle was, and still is, the oxidation of the natural chemicals within the original fabric. In the early days the textile was soaked in sour milk which was expensive and urine which was not quite so dear and more easily available close at hand.

Many people were employed to tour around houses and to collect the urine which was needed in large volumes. After this the material was hung out in the open air in an area known as a 'croft'. To keep the fabric off the ground it was hung on 'tenterhooks'. We still use the phrase today when we are impatient for something to happen.

To the men of cotton the link between 'muck and brass' was acceptable but what they could not tolerate was hold ups in production. They literally wanted to avoid being held up on 'tenterhooks' and good chemists were soon in great demand. John Mercer from Great Harwood was a self-educated former labourer in cotton mills who became an eminent chemist in the late 19th century and made his fortune in the process.

The time of bleaching was halved following the mass production of sulphuric acid in the mid 18th century. This replaced the use of

In the 1960s Dean Farm in Great Harwood was used by the Scouts. It was here in the mid-19th century that a former cotton labourer, John Mercer, became a chemist. 'Mercerisation' was his invention and he also patented red ink.

soured milk. Then came the invention of bleaching powder and thereafter the bleaching process was reduced to only one or two days. This meant a massive increase in the volume of cotton made available not only for home consumption but also for export throughout the world. Soon dyeing machines were devised which involved pressing the fabric between heated copper rollers, a sort of mechanical hot mangle. New rollers were then invented to add a gloss to the fabric.

This led to the development of dyeing and printing on an industrial scale and again Lancashire was in an ideal position to pioneer this process. The way this operated in the workplace was very different from that in the spinning and weaving industry.

The labour force was thus much smaller and the owner tended to live on site and was consequently more closely in touch with his employees. It has been estimated that one firm with less than 300 hands could process half a million yards of dyed cloth in a week. This sort of output would require a workforce of 5,000 spinners and 1,000 weavers.

Joyce Wilkinson, whose husband worked from 1940 to 1973 at a bleach and dyeworks at Stubbins near Ramsbottom, remembers that,

> 'Although the chemicals needed careful handling the work was not as noisy or as dangerous as in spinning and especially weaving mills. Neither there so many workers and the operators spoke regularly to the owners and each knew what the other wanted. Any potential flash points would be sorted out by eye to eye contact on the shop floor.'

Not only were innovations made to dye cotton in a chosen colour, but the printing of patterns soon became modernised and replaced block printing by hand. Credit for mechanised printing is usually accorded to Joseph Lockett of Manchester in 1808. All this meant that Lancashire was unrivalled in the world and for a period of around a century orders poured in to the county.

Chapter 3

The Cotton Workers

The transition from working at home and combining textile production with small scale farming to being employed in a mill and living in the owner's dwelling must have been not only a wrench but also involved some abdication of freedom.

The cottager or the handloom weaver and his family could work as long and as hard as they liked – from sun-up to sunset if they wanted – but their time was their own. The whole family worked together and although even the youngest children laboured away at least they were close to their parents and in some cases to their grandparents. Then came the Industrial Revolution with its strict discipline. All then had to react to the whistle and arrive before the clock determined the closure of the gates. Those latecomers who were locked out were either fined or sacked.

Even in the 1950s working by the clock was still strictly adhered to, as Danny Bellshaw clearly remembers:

'I found that moving from a farm to a mill in Harle Syke near Burnley was a real contrast. Farm animals do not have

The mill clock was feared by latecomers. This one was used at Ellenroad spinning mill from the 1920s until its closure in the 1970s.

watches but they needed looking after and crops had to be tended. We worked daylight hours out of doors and only stopped work when all jobs had been done. When I moved into a cotton mill I came in contact with Billy Mason, the manager. He wore clogs and a flat cap and looked like a boss from the 1850s even though it were 1952. He had a motto: "Waste not want not and never waste owt". I remember his tattered notebook and a little stub of a pencil. Latecomers were noted and duly reported to the boss. It were the first time I were freetened of a clock. I'm still working but I'm back on the land as I work on landscaping at a caravan site in Roughlee. Plants are much easier to deal with than any machine.'

Mary Clegg worked in the same mill as Danny Belshaw but she was devoted to her work as a weaver. She lived in the Stonyholme area of Burnley and travelled daily at first by tram and later on foot to Harle Syke. She recorded her memories in the 1970s and pointed out,

'I worked first on four looms and then on six and had very few accidents but if it were your own fault you were paid nowt. You had to account for your accident both to the union and to the bosses. If both sides agreed then you were given your wages until you were better. This did not happen years ago when nobody gave a thought to the welfare of the cotton workers.'

A feel for the old times can be enjoyed by travelling to Ramsbottom on the East Lancashire Steam Railway which runs from Rawtenstall to Heywood via Ramsbottom and Bury. Look out for the Grants Arms pub and stroll around a largely unspoiled cotton town. The Grants were philanthropic cotton mill owners who became the Cherryble brothers in Charles Dickens' *Nicholas Nickleby*.

There are plenty of academic yet essential accounts of the 'hard times' endured by the cotton workers but there are also accounts of what the operatives themselves thought of conditions. Two things stand out when those who worked in the mills told me of their memories – the truth and the humour.

Spinners

I have family members and friends who worked in the industry, including one who was a mill manager in Burnley in the early 1900s and others who were weavers, spinners, tacklers, twisters, overlookers and engineers.

Cotton in Lancashire could not have achieved world dominance without such an army of workers. One of my friends, Janice Neild, now in her nineties, had a grandfather who was the manager of a spinning mill in Oldham. She told me,

'The old man mentioned that workers arrived in a family group – mum, dad and as many as eight children. If he had to discipline one of 'em they all limped. They were scared to death of the gaffer, especially when trade was slack because how can a family like that change jobs when they live close to the mill in a house rented from the owner? They learned to grin and bear it.'

The profits accrued by cotton mills were directly related to the presence of a large and cheap labour force and in the early days children as young as six were expected to work long hours. The reason for using children as cheap labour was a direct result of power-operated machinery. The sheer strength required to be a male handloom weaver was no longer needed. The machines just needed 'minding' and the spaces between them kept free from dust and debris. Children were ideal for this because their small size allowed them to operate in the confined spaces. At this time most adult workers were on piece rates, thus giving them an incentive to work hard. In contrast children were paid a weekly wage and in the early 1800s we hear of 'little piecers' working in spinning mills. As the children matured they became known as 'big piecers'. Those who worked hard and skilfully eventually became mule spinners.

The weaving mill also had work for children and each skilled loom operator relied on their young tenters, who removed debris and performed errands so that a loom kept running smoothly and without stopping.

Pat Whiteley remembers working at her loom in the 1970s:

'Even then keeping the looms clean was the job of paid adult sweepers and we gave them the benefit of our rough tongue if there was too little or too much oil around and especially when cotton fibres and dust gathered which was always a fire hazard. I remember my mum telling me that in her day they had to clean their own looms and if oil or dust was spotted they were actually fined. Cotton folk all kept their houses spotlessly clean because they were trained to take a pride in being tidy.'

In 2007 Ray Smith, who now lives in Farnworth near Bolton, passed on to me the memories of 99-year-old Jane Nuttall whose whole family worked at Waterfield Mill in Darwen. Her relative, Ernest Lightbown, was an overlooker and many of his weavers were actually family members. He was promoted to overlooker after many years as a competent weaver. Jane clearly remembers the mill celebrations at the time of the Queen's Coronation in 1953.

Weaver and overlooker Ernest Lightbown at Waterfield Mill in Darwen.

*New entrants learning the techniques needed to operate a Lancashire loom
(Pat Whiteley is third from the left on the top row).*

The Abbey Village Mill Christmas party in 1950.

Weavers and overlookers at Waterfield Mill in Darwen,
including Ernest Lightbown.

Initially parents expected children to go to the mill even at the age of five or six because in the handloom weavers' cottages the whole family worked almost from the cradle to the grave. They were used to families working together. Even when they could see that the health of the youngsters was being adversely affected, parents had little alternative but to work their offspring almost to death. There was an insatiable demand for cheap child labour, especially in mills which were some distance from the mill towns. This led to the apprentice scheme, which involved bringing children in from orphanages often as far away as London. The city authorities were glad not to have the expense of keeping these children whilst the mill owners were delighted to have a ready supply of cheap labour.

Some children were housed in appalling conditions but there were a few mill owners who were more enlightened – one fears that these were the exception rather than the rule.

There is a fine example of the apprentice system at Styal Mill on the banks of the river Bollin near Manchester. The mill and its Apprentice House are now ably looked after by the National Trust. Nobody interested in the cotton industry can afford to miss Styal Mill or a study of its archives.

Samuel Greg was born in Belfast but set up businesses in Styal in 1784 and at Caton on the river Lune near Lancaster. Close to the mill at Styal he built a village in order to house workers but even then he found that he could not attract enough labour. For this reason he took advantage of the fact that the poorhouses in the big cities were having to look after too many children and money was in short supply. Greg built what became known as his Apprentice House and this and the vegetable garden associated with it still stand as a reminder of this chapter in the annals of the cotton industry.

Greg's terms were that a parish wishing to 'unload' its surplus children must pay the sum of four guineas and that they should arrive with a supply of clean clothes. Those items listed were two shifts and two frocks for girls or the male equivalent and two brats (aprons). There is no mention of shoes.

In contrast to the conditions at Styal the majority of mill children were very badly treated indeed. As soon as one group of hard worked apprentices were pulled out of their beds to go to work they were replaced by another set of children. It is interesting to note that at Styal the young Thomas Priestley was never asked to work at night but by the 1830s when gas lighting became widely available this was a regular practice – but not at Greg's Mill.

Whilst Styal was an enlightened place, Caton was one aspect of hell. Styal is now a museum whilst the Caton mill has been converted into up-market flats.

In 1802 it was estimated that at least 20,000 apprentices of both sexes were working as mill apprentices. Once steam power replaced water power the demand for this abhorrent form of labour quickly began to disappear. In 1816 an Act was passed which prevented apprentices being sent further than 40 miles from their native parish, but it was really a case of locking the stable door after the horse had bolted.

The old mill at Caton before its conversion into flats.

The most infamous episode of the child apprentice system was at Backbarrow near Ulverston. The youngsters were so badly treated there that many died and their bodies were 'disposed of' to avoid controversy. Later the mill was turned over to the production of 'Dolly Blue' by the Reckitts Company. I explored this mill on several occasions as my schoolfriend's mother worked at the blue works. She would come home looking like an ancient Briton covered in woad. Even in the 1940s local folk still told tales of the ghosts of ill-treated apprentices which haunted the old mills.

Not all children were as badly treated as some of these tiny apprentices. I had not expected to find a person who had family memories dating back to Arkwright but I was lucky. Few families have cotton memories going back so far as Meg Hartnell's. Meg, who now lives in Marlborough in Wiltshire, recalls:

'My great-great-grandmother was born in Bootle near Liverpool in 1862 and started work at the age of eight at Old Leigh's Mill. She continued to work in the mill until she was 72! She started work at 6 am and had breakfast between 8 and 8.30 am. She had one hour for dinner and finished work at 6 pm. On Saturdays they finished work at noon. She remembered a single mother who took her baby to work and put her in one of the bogies, which were small waggons on wheels and where the big bobbins were kept. She also told of the problems faced during the American Cotton Famine. The first cotton which arrived after the war was over was greeted by cheers and some women came out of their houses and kissed the consignment.'

Weavers

If the spinning mills were male dominated, the weaving mills were very much the province of women, although the men tended to fill the positions of managers, craftsmen and engineers.

Pat Whiteley, who only retired as a weaver in the 1980s, remembers her roots which were on the female side:

'When I was young I wanted to be a nurse but you had to be eighteen before you started training. So at sixteen my mum got me into the mill and I learned to weave under her guidance. I enjoyed this so much that I stayed in the mill all my working life. In the 1940s, however, each mill including mine at Ewood close to Blackburn Rovers Football Ground organised its own training courses and I still treasure a photograph that I have of this first introductory week. Like other mothers, mine then taught me to weave by sharing her looms. We all had to learn quickly because having a trainee at the looms meant a loss of income because we were all on piece work. I remember my pride when I was allowed to work my own looms and calculate my own earnings.'

Mrs I. Chadwick of West View, Blackburn also has a family tradition in cotton and wrote:

'My family worked in the weaving mills in Darwen, including the famous India Mill. I have photographs showing family members taken in the 1920s but like many people nobody remembered to write down the names. I know that at one time three generations of female Chadwicks worked in the same mill and mum's aunts and even grandmothers trained the young lasses who were soon made into grand weavers.'

Mavis Eccles of Branch Road in Blackburn, now well into her eighties, relayed to me the memories of her 92-year-old brother Fred Bates who now lives at Henley-in-Arden:

'Many of our local mills had nicknames which were a sign of the affection folk had for their local workspot. Griffin Mill, for example, was known as the "Physic" because one of its directors was the local Dr Lees. A mill near the old cemetery was known as the "Button Shop" because it was

Some of Mrs I. Chadwick's family who worked in the Darwen Mills in the early 20th century

the first to have a push button electric start. In the Mill Hill area there was "Aht o' seet" (Out of Sight) Mill because it was set away from the main road along a back alley. Imperial Mill, one of the biggest in the town was known as the "Twelve Apostles" because there were twelve directors on the board. Then there was "T'Mushroom" because it was built so quickly that local folk suggested that it had sprouted up overnight! The mill at Bower House Fold in the Mill Hill district had a particularly smoky chimney and was known as "The Smut".'

Peter Riley also told me of the 'Mushroom', which was also known as the 'Mush'; its actual name was Albert Mill, once owned by Lucas Ltd. It was demolished in the 1970s and is now Green Park Housing Estate. He showed me a photograph of the Blackburn factory lasses each carrying a shuttle.

Mrs Roberts, who lives in the charmingly named Besses o' th' Barn, near Bury, also has memories of her life in the mills and the nicknames they were sometimes given:

'I left school at 15, starting work at Textile No 3 in Farnworth, near Bolton. It also had two other names – 'Little Tec' and 'Zeppelin Shed'. A Zeppelin had dropped a bomb on the town during World War I. Everyone knew where you worked if you mentioned any of those names. My first job in the mill was a doffer in the mule spinning room (happy times), there was four of us.

'I worked in there for twelve months, then we had to move into the cone winding room but my heart belonged to the spinning room. I stayed in there for twelve months then sadly my mother died and I went to live down Radcliffe, near Bury. Then I got a job at Woodhouse Hambleys as a battery filler for an automatic loom. There was twelve weavers in that room and myself. They all loved me because I was very fast. They all called me Speedy. I worked there for a while then I moved nearer home. Then I got myself a job in the Pioneer Mills in Radcliffe working in the towel room. Parcelling towels up and packing them ready to go out on the wagons. In between that I got married and had a family, moving to Besses o' th' Barn Mill. Then I got myself a job working 5.30 to 9.30 cone winding at the Newcona Mill in Besses. I stayed there for nine years until it closed. Then a year later a new firm took it over. This was South Lancs Winding Co. and I worked as a cone winder. They installed a knitting machine which made dishcloths but none of us had ever seen one before so we all had a stint on it.

'I didn't last very long as my dishcloths were full of holes and they had to go out as seconds. I stayed at South Lancs for about twelve years till it closed down in 1982. So that's my working life in the cotton mills. It went on a reet long time.'

These nicknames survived over the generations and were still known as demolition began, often as late as the 1970s. The mill workers had an affection for their mill and for the work they did. In view of the fact that their work was hard and the pay was low it is a surprise that industrial relations were not so aggressive as was the case in other industries.

There were in most mills regular training sessions which brought all workers including bosses up to date with newly adapted machinery. This did a lot to help industrial relations and Eric Goddan of Briefield near Burnley remembers:

'I attended these sessions from being a lad to the time I was a manager. We were all in the same job after all. Money were always tight and I still remember an awld chap called

Eric Goddan (first right) being shown new technological improvements to a loom in the 1960s.

Maurice Albert at a time when we finished work at 5 pm. The awld lad always went to the hot water boiler and filled two big flasks. One was for his shaving and washing up water and the other for his brews of tea at night. He also cooked his regular meal of black puddings by keeping the right side of the boiler man. Everybody was keen on saving brass but there was not often real arguments with regard to wages in the 1950s. Most were too glad to be in work.'

There was not always 'trouble in t'mill, Mr Arkwright', as the chapter which follows well proves.

Chapter 4

Trade Unions

Whilst the writers and political thinkers of the 18th century were beginning to denounce the evils of the developing factory system, the workers themselves were trying to obtain rights and privileges and not just operating as virtual slaves who were given a pittance disguised as wages.

The cotton workers were at the forefront of this press for change as the countryside was swamped under a blanket of buildings and the smoke which they created. For the first time the humble worker had to function by the clock rather than by the sun. In winter most would not even see the daylight and within a single lifetime the smell of fresh air had become a memory.

The Oldham Friendly Society of Associated Cotton Spinners was formed as early as 1797, the word 'friendly' here indicated that this was a convivial meeting point with no militant edge to it. In 1829 there was an attempt under the leadership of John Doherty to combine all workers in textiles under the banner of his 'Grand General Union'. This would have involved the 'wool men' of Yorkshire working together with the 'cotton men' of

Lancashire, but the time was not right and such a union was never cemented. The workers were far too parochial and reacted to their own employer rather than to a distant organisation which they would have to pay for. Money was tight enough as it was, and outspoken workers would not be employed by the local mill owners.

There was a giant leap forwards in Rochdale when the operatives resented employers paying part of their wages in food and other goods. These items were often expensive and of inferior quality. Many employers did this in order to reduce the real value of wages. So it was that in 1844 the workers formed a society which they named 'The Rochdale Pioneers'. To start with, the rest of the textile towns regarded the Pioneers as a joke and christened them 'The Weavers' Dream'. The movement, however, went from strength to strength and by combining resources they could purchase high standard goods at fair prices. The workers were rewarded by accounts being kept of how much they spent. At periodic intervals a small percentage of their spend was returned to the shopper. What became known as the CWS (Co-operative Wholesale Society) 'divi' was a vital part of shopping for more than a century.

The Pioneer venture took off and first Oldham, then Manchester, Liverpool and Birmingham followed Rochdale's lead. The CWS's huge headquarters is now based in Manchester and also covers banking and insurance. Their motto was that it would protect the workers from the cradle to the grave and the CWS still offers a funeral service. Their sales outlets still prosper and are more ethically based than many supermarket chains.

The Co-op movement was indeed just a pioneer but the real rise of trade unionism dates from the 1850s. As early as 1847 there was a demand by cotton workers for a 10% pay rise. It is not surprising at this point to note that there was some confusion. The mill owners did not have a regular wage policy amongst themselves and obviously neither had their workforce. So it was that some mills granted 10% and others did not.

Everything came to a head in the Preston area during 1853, when events turned really ugly. Some masters refused any form of compromise not just over wages but also over conditions of employment.

Neither side would move and so the mill owners 'locked out' more than 20,000 workers. The owners obviously wanted to keep their mills running and so they brought in what became known as 'knobsticks'. These were poor people from the countryside and from Ireland shipped in to do the work. Those locked out were determined to fight the men that they termed the 'Cotton Lords of Preston'. This strife went on for 36 weeks and into 1854 but the Lords won as their workers' families began to starve.

This then was a situation in which the masters were still on one side and the workers on the other. Neither side would ever again trust the other and the events of Preston first spread to the cotton towns and then to other workers throughout the rest of Britain.

In 1867, after the Cotton Famine eased following the events of the American Civil War, a Royal Commission was appointed to examine the development of trade unions. One member of this commission was Thomas Hughes (1822-1896), the author of *Tom Brown's Schooldays*. It was recommended that the benefits of a trade union (really an advanced form of the medieval guilds) should not just be available to skilled workers but also to unskilled operatives. It took some time for this to be put into operation but it developed into an invaluable trend. The influence of this welcome wind of change was felt in the older craft unions, which at last began to follow the efficiencies brought about by new machinery.

The cotton operatives were finally finding some improvement in their working conditions. An Amalgamated Association of Card and Blowing Room Operatives was formed in 1886 and this was followed in the 1890s by the Amalgamated Weavers' Association.

The employers soon realised that their workers were becoming too powerful and set up their own Master Cotton Spinners' Association. The two sides had to meet face to face sooner rather than later. The operatives were represented by James Mawdsley,

In 1840, two cotton workers died in clashes with the military at Preston

one of the tough guys of the Master Cotton Spinners' Association, and the employers were represented by Sir Charles Macara. A six-week strike had been rumbling in 1893 when the two met at the Brooklands Hotel which, probably deliberately, was sited on the Cheshire side of Manchester and away from the areas of conflict.

It was here that the now famous Brooklands Agreement was signed. This resulted in the setting up of three courts, one of which was described as a 'first instance' meeting and the other two relating to an appeal structure. In reality it meant that no dispute should allow either a lockout by the employers or a strike entered into by the workers until all of these tribunals had met and failed to find an agreement. These days we would call these courts 'arbitrations' and it worked so well that there were no significant stoppages in the cotton industry for a period of sixteen years.

This is a tribute to the Brooklands Agreement but it also coincided with a period when the Lancashire cotton industry was at its more profitable, wages were guaranteed and expansion was going on at a phenomenal rate. For some reason the Brooklands Agreement was replaced by what turned out to be a much less flexible Industrial Council.

Both sides – employers and workers – have had to accept that the bigger the organisation the more difficult it is to organise. This did lead to a polarisation in industrial relations during the events of the First World War and especially after the Russian Revolution of 1917. The communist ideology in Britain made industrial relations much worse. Trade unions became more demanding of the employers and the latter more tyrannical with regard to their own workers. Some unions were urging a revolution in the Russian style, but it also has to be admitted that without them many mill owners would have trodden their workers under foot. If trade unions had not already existed in the Cotton County in the early 1920s, it would have been necessary to invent them!

In the 1950s my historian friend Eric Riley wrote a thesis on the Mechanics' Institutes which were spawned from artisans working in engineering and courses were held by the Workers' Education Association (WEA). Many Mechanics' Institute buildings still exist although serving different functions. The Institute close to the Town Hall in Burnley is now a thriving entertainment complex and an integral part of the conservation area.

Obviously the mill owners had their own clubs where business could be conducted and many were also influential Freemasons. Some of the cotton operatives reacted by setting up their own clubs. On a side street close to the parish church in Colne is the still functional Tacklers' Club. Here the relative working practices of the owners could be discussed and wage rates compared.

It was inevitable that the unions and bosses would have their ups and downs but usually there was give and take on both sides, along with a dry sense of humour so typical of Lancashire folk in general. All this came out as I spoke at length to Rex Gormley, who lives in the Cherry Tree area of Blackburn:

'We were taught about our union rights from our first day in the mill. I began work as a weaving apprentice in 1950 and as first one mill closed and then another I worked all ower the shop. I were at several mills in Blackburn including Longshaw, Highfield, Malverden and Robinson and Seeds. I moved to Bamber Bridge and Colne in search of work and finished up at Roe Lee in Blackburn. I was determined to get on and went to night school to broaden my knowledge and this led to promotion to tackler and then into the office. I was also elected to the union and this gave me a dilemma. I could not be a boss and a union fella at the same time even though it gave me a balanced view. Sometimes unionists would be very balanced because they had a chip on each shoulder.

'As a tackler I learned to get to know my weavers and I even had nicknames for some of them. There was 'I need thee every hour' who was not very competent and neither was 'Where the 'ell is 'ee'. Then there was 'Ciggy' who was always nipping out for a fag. There was 'Gravestones', who had bad teeth caused mainly through kissing the shuttle and 'Miss World' who had big busts but refused to wear a bra and she kept swinging these dangerously close to her looms. The weavers called me 'Rex Mouse' because I always kept mice and rats away from the alleys. The rodents urinated on the shuttles and of course until later times the weavers all sucked the thread through the shuttle.'

Rex also had memories of tussles with the old mill-owning families and their promotion of friends and family, but he was not bitter about all of them:

'It's only natural for the boss to look after his kids and those of his relatives. I did not mind providing they worked hard and were good at their jobs. Union men like me have to be honest and admit that those on our side of the fence did the same thing. I remember one serious confrontation when I was a very senior worker and I had to point out that some weavers were being paid well below the minimum rate. I was told to shut up and offered a back hander to flout the union I was a member of. I could not do that but I knew that the profit margins were so low that if they increased the wages they would go bust and nobody would have a job. I was in such a stew but I was lucky and got a job in another mill, which was not easy in the 1970s.

'Eventually more and more mills were forced to close and in 1981 I decided to retire and I am now more than a little bit deaf and my chest is none too good after years of breathing cotton dust. There were times when the whole mill looked like heavy snow was falling. Did I enjoy it? Of course I did and we all need to celebrate the work we did. I also enjoyed the union work which often involved going to summer school which always took place in holiday times so that I lost no work. I learned about the

Kirk and Company, shuttle makers at Blackburn, 1900.

complicated industrial relations from when the unions first tried to develop right up to the time when I retired. I like to think that I understood both sides but those early workers certainly got a rough deal.

'Accidents, both major and minor, were a feature of all mills which were full of moving parts. Most owners refused to pay compensation although a few paid the wages of folk until they returned to work. The worker, however, had to prove that they were not negligent or in a place where they weren't supposed to be. Even the union officials were careful not to upset the bosses who kept them in work, and were not always on the side of the victim. I remember in the 1960s suggesting that as the union had solicitors they should decide on the merits of each case. In the Union Lodge my suggestion was carried but only by the margin of one vote! These days litigation is a bloody hobby with some folk and it has gone too far but sometimes the cotton workers did not go half far enough to make use of existing laws.'

The real decline in cotton actually began at the end of the First World War and employers have been blamed because they failed to invest in new machinery involving changes in technology. The trade unions, however, have to take their share of blame. Spinners and weavers had ever more powerful unions intent on protecting existing work patterns which were often not cost effective and were resistant to change.

Employers were still making profits but from 1918 they made constant and often unrealistic attempts to drive down wages. One

Trafalgar Mill, Burnley about 1900 – note the children known as 'half-timers'.

cannot expect wage reductions at the same time as higher prices for food: 1919 saw the first ever strike by all cotton workers acting more or less in unison. The unions had two main aims, both of which seem reasonable at least in the modern context. All operatives wanted to work a basic 48-hour week, but providing they were paid extra, overtime would be welcomed. In addition to this the half-time system was to be abolished, which had been discussed since the Education Act of 1870.

The half-timer system was just that – a child, sometimes called a *tenter*, would attend school for half a day and then labour in a mill for the rest of the day.

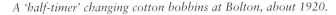

A 'half-timer' changing cotton bobbins at Bolton, about 1920.

In 1970 I had a conversation with Maureen Barnes, a Burnley weaver who was born in 1884, and who told me:

> 'One week I were at school in t'mornin' and at work till th'afternoon. When I started in 1895 I were nobbut eleven but when my sister were old enough in 1900 half-timers could only be set on at twelve. I remember being given a green card and teachers or overlookers at the mill had to sign to say we had turned up to both spots. I started at 6 in t'mornin' and finished around 8 at neet. God, it were tirin'.'

This half-time system continued throughout the First World War and was only officially abolished in 1918. Actually the ban was not fully implemented until 1921 in Lancashire, probably as a direct result of a 1919 strike.

Soldiers who returned from the Front remembered the senseless carnage and at times inhuman discipline of the military. When they returned to work they resented bosses and overlookers who had not been to war, especially when they treated the returning workers with disdain. They were already disillusioned when the employers decided in April 1922 to reduce wages by 40% and then in October the rates were cut by a further 10%. It is small wonder that trade unions gained ground and men were eager to accept the premise that 'Unity is Strength'.

The 1926 General Strike, which was ruthlessly crushed, did not help. Once the employers thought that the workers' strength had been sapped, they took on an even more belligerent stance. They began to try to curtail traditional craft controls and ensure that the mill managers and overlookers had even more power.

This meant that the traditional union unity was eroded as employers began to compete amongst themselves for profits, driving down wages and causing even more discontent among workers trying hard to make a living and at the same time maintain their dignity. No worker wanted to strike but at times they were given little option. Some writers have noted that following the General Strike of 1926 things quietened down to a period of peace. An armed truce might be a better description, especially in East Lancashire.

Burnley employers, for example, instigated what became known as the 'More Looms' system. This meant that one weaver had to operate eight looms instead of four and this reduced the wages bill substantially. The unions reacted by agreeing to operate the system, always providing that the 'More Looms' operators were all men. They made the suggestion that women should leave the cotton industry and take jobs as domestic servants. It is hardly surprising that this led to a hostile swing to the political left. Nelson became known as 'Little Moscow' and the unions there were certainly more powerful than in other towns. This was because Nelson was weaving a fine cloth which was less affected by a recession than towns like Blackburn which concentrated upon the production of basic cloth for the Indian market. Bolton too suffered less of a recession because the town had a variety of engineering factories including the nearby Horwich Steam Locomotive works.

In 1931 the Blackburn unemployment rate increased and in some of the smaller towns the figure reached as high as 60%. Between 1929 and 1939 the Blackburn population declined by 17,538. By 1937 Lancashire's production of cotton fabric was around 50% of the figure for 1912 and even the most optimistic could not visualise this decline being halted.

Between the First and Second World Wars around 800 cotton mills were closed down and successive governments did very little to help. Indeed the only time that Westminster seemed to sympathise with the cotton trade was during the lead up to an election.

The major cause of the demise of Lancashire cotton was the rising cost of labour. The profit during the height of the Industrial Age was due to the almost limitless supply of cheap labour. Children who came into the mills as half-timers were not paid for several months and only then if they were considered to be competent. If they were mule spinners they became known as 'little piecers' and they could remain in this humble and poorly paid position until they were 25 or a male spinner retired. After 25, if no 'man's job' was on hand, they became known as 'side piecers'. Some reached almost 40 before a 'proper job' became available.

Many women weavers spoke respectfully to their bosses as their daughters approached working age. The girl worked at her mother's side and this was initially a problem because weavers were paid at piece rates. The learner slowed down the production of the teacher but once the two were weaving together each with their own looms the family fortunes recovered.

What finally condemned Lancashire to the role of a minor world cotton supplier came at the end of the Second World War with the rise of the compulsory school leaving age. In all respects this has to be regarded as a good thing but it did mean that countries

What would our modern-day laws make of transporting this load from the 1930s?

which still relied on child labour could easily undercut the Lancashire prices.

The Lancashire cotton industry did not suddenly disappear, though all prophets could see that the writing was on the wall. Technical colleges still developed and improved already existing courses relating to advances in spinning, weaving, finishing and textile machinery. As early as January 1927 Pitman's launched a fortnightly magazine in 30 parts. This was called the *Textile Educator* and it cost 1s 3d per issue. This stimulated the growth in the number and skills of textile operators and from the late 1920s up to the present day Lancashire has maintained its pool of knowledge regarding textiles. Nowadays it is mainly local history classes which continue these basic skills. There has been some spin-off into the woollen industry, which because of some home-produced raw materials has not been so devastated as has been the case with cotton.

Even when the Second World War was becoming inevitable little thought was given with regard to the effect that conflict would have on the cotton industry. Considering what happened to cotton imports during the First World War, this lack of foresight is inexcusable. Perhaps we can also understand why no plans were made to preserve the Lancashire cotton industry at the end of the Second World War.

At the start of the war some efforts were made towards maintaining all our imports and exports. Then came the fall of France and later the Nazi occupation of Holland, Denmark and especially Norway. This meant that the German navy and the U-boats in particular had captured ports from which they could disrupt the major British trade routes.

By 1941 the ports of Liverpool and Manchester were too busy maintaining food supplies to worry over much about cotton. The understandable government reaction was to 'restrict' the employment of mills. They kept some in full operation whilst others were closed. This obviously saved on coal. These vast areas of roofed spaces were too good to miss and many mills became munitions storage areas, or food stores for use when invasion looked likely. Around one third of the mills were closed and for this some compensation was paid. All this complex planning was under the remit of the Cotton Controller.

Obviously priority was given to mills which produced military equipment including uniforms, bandages and camouflage netting. In September 1941 the Utility Clothing Scheme came into operation and many mills were thus occupied.

After the war the British government made another error. They assumed that there would be a great demand for cotton goods and that a high proportion of this would be supplied by Lancashire. This turned out not to be the case. The United States, India and a re-equipped Japan were in the market. They had new machines and more modern working practices.

Three commissions were set up in Lancashire in 1946. These were the Evershed Commission overseeing mule spinning, whilst the Aronson Commission took a close look at the more modern ring spinning and carding processes. Then there was the Cotton Manufacturing Commission whose brief was to rationalise the Lancashire loom weaving machinery.

This meant changes in old and long established working practices, which the unions were reluctant to abandon. Despite the Commissioners pointing out to the unions the acute competition they were facing, they still threatened strike action and in 1946 the working hours were reduced from 48 to 45 hours. This would only inflate prices and the Labour Government at the time fully realised that export production targets had to be met.

One solution was to open more mills and employ more women. Indeed there was even a suggestion to conscript women but this was thought to be political suicide as an election was looming. The solution was therefore to encourage people from India and Pakistan to immigrate to the Lancashire towns and fill this labour shortage.

A further problem for the Lancashire cotton industry came in 1952 when the world cotton trade overestimated demand and first prices fell even further and then came a slump. It was felt even more in Lancashire where labour costs were higher. This meant that some cotton workers were more often out of work than in it, as Marlene Jaques remembers:

'There was a worry every Friday morning when lists went up to see if the mill was working the following week. Dad came home to his dinner and so did I from school. There was obviously worry when the list said that he was 'playing' the next week. I didn't really understand the implications, all I knew was that Dad would have tea ready when I got home from school and that was good. How they managed to make ends meet I do not know but I never seemed to have worries. I went to ballet lessons and my grammar school and guides uniforms were always as good as those worn by other girls. I went on all school holidays. The 'laying off' led to inter-mill rivalry. Mother had a draper's shop on Abel Street in Burnley which was in the heart of 'weaver land'. All the lasses would come in for their 'cross-over' aprons and headscarves for work and their silk and lisle stockings for weekend. They all came in with their gossip and would report on which mill was working or which was playing – Shackleton or Ferndale, Cameron or Elm Street all around the town.'

Norah Bennet who now lives in Brighton remembers the rivalry of firms in Preston:

'My uncle worked for Hawkins Cottons in Preston. In 1953 the company bought "Douglas", which was the name given to a large van fitted out with shelves. This toured all over the country selling the company goods and they kept working long after other companies had had to close.'

The period between 1958 and 1975 saw the real decline in Lancashire textiles, at which time I was teaching in Bolton and Burnley but with lots of family friends and neighbours feeling the crunch of the cotton decline. This will be the subject of chapter 7.

Exports were falling and government pressure was on to 'rationalise'. This meant small firms amalgamating and long

'Douglas', the first of Hawkins Sales and Publicity vans was put on the road in June 1953. Touring the country districts, it enabled customers and others to see the quality and variety of its goods.

established family firms being taken over by large conglomerates such as Courtaulds and ICI. By 1971 only 5% of men in Lancashire were textile workers and only 6% of women. In many cases, cotton was being replaced by man-made fibres.

The fewer the workers, the less powerful the unions became and the large companies were free to impose their own working conditions. Once these huge multi-national companies got control of the mills it was easy to relocate the whole business to countries where the labour costs were only a fraction of those in Lancashire.

I felt this still to be relevant when in the autumn of 2006 I visited Mrs Davies, who had worked as a wages clerk at the Hilden Mills in Oswaldtwistle. She told me, 'The company is moving some of its operations to Egypt and so I'll retire. That really is something to write about. I'm redundant for the first time in my life at the age of 93!' Sadly, Mrs Davies died in 2007.

It is fascinating to record that the Hilden Company is run by the Hargreaves family who, as already mentioned, are descendants of James, the inventor of the spinning jenny. Lancashire cotton does now seem to be hanging by a thread and its history has come full circle.

Peter Hargreaves lamented:

'All Lancashire cotton manufacturers over the last 30 years have been faced with overwhelming foreign competition and in 2007 we were faced with our most worrying problem. Should we close down altogether or move our production abroad where costs were lower? What we did was to move our production base to Egypt but to operate our offices from Oswaldtwistle. Our sales is still a UK-based operation and the quality of our product has not been compromised. Our customers, including most of the world's airlines, have remained with us. You can imagine the logistical problem we faced in shipping all our heavy machinery to Egypt. We have also relocated many of our managerial staff and Hilden is as British as it is possible to be given the current financial climate.'

His words, if no others, inspired me to set down the history of the Cotton County. This phase in our history should never be forgotten and neither should the county's influence in other textile regions of the world which owe much to Lancashire's history and expertise.

Chapter 5

Wakes Weeks and Resorts

To the folk of Lancashire, the government decision in 2006 to rationalise school terms and holidays meant the end of a valued tradition of the cotton industry – the Wakes weeks. Elsie Slater of Bolton, now aged 96 and living in the same house where she was born, summed up their feelings:

'We all lived, worked and loved cotton and them Wakes weeks were a treat. We saved up all year to go to Blackpool and we knew that only Bolton folk would be there. Once we left, usually stony broke, it were time for another town like Oldham, Rochdale or Burnley. Our landlady loved it because she was sure of visitors all through the summer. Now there will be a feight as us and folk from the south all compete for overseas holidays at the same time. I'm knockin' on too much these days but I still went to Blackpool on my Wakes week until I were 93! The Wakes holidays certainly kept prices down because there were plenty of competition over the whole of t' summer.'

Railways were the key to Wakes travel from the 1890s onwards. When the Midland Railway amalgamated to set up the LMS (London, Midland and Scottish), the Lakes Specials were always full to the brim.

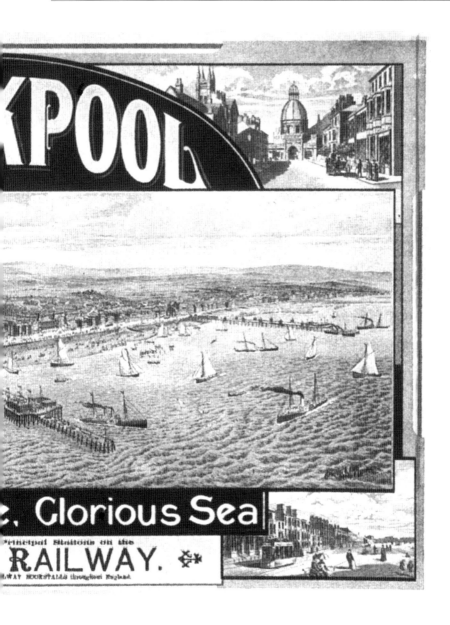

Bernice Simmons also remembers her Wakes holidays, as the mill workers from Abbey Village between Bolton and Blackburn packed up and 'got weaving' to Blackburn station: 'We went to Blackpool and we took food with us and the owners of the boarding houses cooked it for us. It goes without saying that we used to "camp" with other families during our stay but we all took care to talk about Blackpool and not about the mill, except on the last day which none of us enjoyed.'

A 'wake' originally indicated a funeral and this could be an excuse for a party, which if the master was rich often involved a day's holiday with pay. Some historians, however, have suggested that the wake may have originated as a 'rush bearing', when local people gathered sweet-smelling rushes and spread them in the church. They were rewarded with free food and drink and a holiday which may have spread into two days. Some towns like Littleborough near Rochdale have revived this tradition and it is hoped that the event will spread to other parts of the county.

When the textile workers were first given holidays it was initially only for a few days so that machinery could be overhauled and mill chimneys and boilers repaired and kept clean. Industrialists soon realised that to have every Lancashire mill idle at the same time made no economic sense and there would be a shortage of skilled men to do the maintenance. The idea of staggered holidays over the towns in the county soon evolved and the seaside watering holes became known as the Wakes Resorts. These holiday weeks worked well until a two week annual holiday was negotiated and then a degree of overlapping took place.

Sheila Parker remembers these times vividly:

'Our family were not well off and even when we got two weeks' holiday we could only afford to go to Blackpool for one week. During the second week we went walking in the local countryside around Rochdale. We always went to Hollingworth Lake which was built to provide watter for t'Rochdale canal. You could sail on the lake and there were amusements all round it. It were known to all on us as t'weavers' seaport.'

Sheila recalls that many people were unable to go away for even one week. The local coach firms supplied an alternative. They organised day trips. Brenda Dickinson of Burnley recalls:

'We would all go to Duke Bar where several charas (charabancs) set off to all sorts of places. You could go to Blackpool, Morecambe, Southport, and once we even went to Llangollen in Wales.'

Joan Proctor of Blackburn remembers how busy the station was at the start of a Wakes week, when the Blackpool special steamed and clanked up to the platform:

Charabanc trips were organised from about 1912 onwards. Later, luxury coaches replaced the 'charas'.

'You could book the train in advance, but there were no reserved seats and the "specials" were always overcrowded. Those who managed to find seats put cases on them and the children perched on the luggage. There were no corridors in those days and each carriage had a rack made of wood and rope. Luggage could be stored on the rack and even small children would be put up on the rack and often slept peacefully during the journey. The cases were also used as tables for picnics or even for playing cards on.'

As the mill towns' claustrophobic atmosphere faded into the distance all eyes turned to a greener countryside and then there was a competition for who was the first to spot Blackpool Tower. Staying in hotels was only for the posh folk and the workers stayed in boarding houses. There was a tradition that the same house was booked year after year.

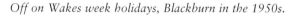

Off on Wakes week holidays, Blackburn in the 1950s.

Not everybody went to Blackpool and there were other resorts which had rival attractions. Southport, Fleetwood and Morecambe were all popular whilst those who could afford a cruise went to the Isle of Man. Wilfred Jaques had fond memories of Southport:

> 'My father was a mill manager and a bit posh to go to Blackpool and as a young man I got to love Morecambe, but especially Southport. So much so that when I got married I went to Southport for my honeymoon. It was always regarded as a "posh" version of Blackpool and always had a refined feel to it and still has.'

Some families had more adventurous holidays even though close to the traditional resorts. Betty Beardsworth, who still lives in Rishton where she was born, wrote to me:

> 'We used to go to a caravan site near St Annes and next to the old Guide House Hotel at Warton. This has now been demolished although the site is still there and our family have memories of the area from the 1930s until well into the 1950s. This was once the base of the Guides who shepherded people in row boats or on foot along the sandy estuary of the river Ribble. When I was a little girl I would walk down to the Ribble and near the hotel buy sweets from an elderly lady called Miss Kershaw who ran a little shop. I still treasure a postcard bought from her and showing that the Guide House was still busy.'

Wilfred Jaques also spent many holidays in caravans:

> 'Once we could afford a car we went further afield. On one occasion we went to Cornwall with several friends. We went in two cars travelling in convoy. We arranged to keep in touch by meeting up at RAC boxes. These were all numbered. We had an ornate RAC badge on the front of the car and as we passed the patrolmen they would salute us – all very grand.'

101

Blackpool during Blackburn Wakes weeks, July 1967.

Jimmy Jaques, a Burnley mill manager, on his Wakes holiday at Morecambe.

All these memories prove that each resort had, and still has, its own character and this also applies to the mill towns themselves. I spoke to numerous people and their memories show the individuality of each cotton town.

Jean Brocklebank has family memories of old Accrington from the 1870s to the present time:

'My mum, dad and all grandparents worked in the cotton mills around Accrington and Oswaldtwistle but three of my uncles worked in other industries. Fred worked at the Ewbank factory which made carpet sweepers, whilst George and Terry worked all their lives at Howard and Bullough who made machinery associated with the cotton industry. My mum told me about going away for the Wakes. We crowded onto trams which took us to the station. On one occasion coming home they had no brass left and had to walk home which was three miles from the station. It was raining and the cases were heavy.'

I have very happy memories of Bacup as I have often given lectures to the 'Bacup Nats'. This club has an associated museum and this is the place to see lots of memorabilia relating to the cotton and other industries including coal mining. One of my uncles was a brass band player and he told me that the Irwell Springs band was one of the most renowned in Britain. The town cricket team was often made up of mill workers and hard-earned wages were invested by thousands of keen spectators.

In contrast to compact little Bacup, Blackburn was a huge town which earned a goodly living from cotton and its associated industries such as foundries and machine making.

Michael Dawson, whose grandfather worked for Clayton and Goodfellow, which was a Blackburn steam engine and boiler works, takes up the story:

'The old man told me years ago that too many folk believe that inventors died out with Arkwright but this was not

The Wonderful Wakes. Darwen's station platform is crowded with holidaymakers and their luggage – every shape, size and age imagainable. c. 1900

true. New improvements and efficiencies were being worked on all the time. New designs for pistons, valves and even the rope designs which were attached to the winding wheels were being invented all the time. Once the idea was converted into a drawing, fitters and turners like grandad had to work to achieve very accurate and consistent tolerances. For cotton mills to run there had to be huge back up services and when history books are written these essentials are not usually considered.'

Blackburn's textile history goes back long before the age of cotton as I discovered a few years ago when I interviewed Maggie Simms, the curator of Blackburn Museum. She mentioned that,

'The river Blakewater runs through the town and is a tributary of the river Darwen. There's always an argument with regard to how it gets its name. Some think that it was a Black-water which was peat stained as it flowed down from the hills. Others think that it was Bleach-water because long before cotton, flax was bleached before being processed into linen. Whatever the reason Blackburn was an important textile centre from Anglo-Saxon times onwards.'

It is not fair to link Blackburn with Darwen because each has its own unique character. Darwen, like Blackburn, exported much of its cotton to the Asian sub-continent and it is no accident that the chimney of India Mill still dominates the town even though it is not associated with cotton anymore.

Nobody has clearer memories than Mrs Audrey Blinkinsopp, now well into her nineties and living in Brisbane, Australia. She has still not lost her broad Lancashire accent:

'I were a reet Darraner and I were a weaver at India Mill. My granfer towd me that he remembers when the bellman went round t'streets mekin' sure nobody were late. I were at India Mill in 1931 when Gandhi visited the town on what were called "a fact finding job" but he was really spying to see if cotton could be med cheaper in India which was what happened a few years later. People came to see 'im all dressed in white robes and curryin' a spinnin' wheel. People would have paid to see 'im because we knew nowt about politics in them days.'

Old and proud Lancastrians also still insist on placing Bury, Oldham and Rochdale in Lancashire and refuse to acknowledge the existence of Greater Manchester. Oldham was among the first of the towns to embrace King Cotton and as early as 1845 there were more than 200 mills employing around 16,000 people, while by 1866 the population was around 80,000 and rising. It has been calculated that more than three million spindles were clattering away and much brass and even more muck and pollution was being produced.

There was a real rivalry among the cotton towns and feelings reached a climax when the Cotton Queen was crowned. Each town elected their most beautiful lass and, during the summer, the overall queen was crowned. The girl, her town and her mill could then bask in glory until the next year. The winner in 1926, for example, was Edna Taylor of Oldham.

Writing up these memories set me in search of the notes I made when talking at some length and on many occasions with Dame Thora Hird. We talked cotton and Wakes and on one occasion she waxed really lyrical:

'I was born and bred in Morecambe and it was here that I was determined to become an actress. The man who became my husband had a dance band in the town. Scottie was a reet grand chap and we worked as equals. This was also the case as the holiday crowds came into the town during the 1950s. They were families and very often their purse strings were pulled by the women. I remember one woman from Burnley telling me that before they set off she

The crowning of the Burnley Cotton Queen in the 1920s.

put money for rent and food in an Oxo tin and buried this "in t'coil oil". They could then spend up knowing that there was enough brass to keep them going until the family mill money started to come in again.'

The history of Burnley's cotton weaving industry and the Wakes weeks are graphically told in the excellent Weavers' Triangle museum and this is the place to enjoy a snack and soak up a fascinating chapter of Lancashire's cotton memories. Of all the cotton towns, with regard to the holiday week Burnley was unique. The holiday period was, and still is, remembered as Burnley Fair and there are vivid depictions of this in the Weavers' Triangle museum. For those not going away a fun fair was organised but there was also a 'pot fair' where cheap stalls were set up selling pottery and porcelain.

An even more famous museum than the Weavers' Triangle is to be found in the Helmshore Mills Textile Museum, which has

Edna Taylor of Oldham was crowned Cotton Queen in 1926.

Off on a Wakes holiday, Burnley's Parker Lane in the 1940s.

machines dating from the very early days of the Industrial Revolution. I discovered this history during several discussions with Ian Gibson, who has been the man responsible for the very recent refurbishment of the museum. Ian told me,

'Actually, this is not one textile museum but two and we can trace the whole history of the industry from the beginnings to its demise in the 1980s. I always tell people to start in the mill built in the 18th century which processed wool. Here we have examples of all the machines which can actually work. We have the only working Arkwright water frame in the world and we also have cotton spinning material dating to the 1960s. This deals with spinning but visitors are then directed to go to Burnley and explore the Queen Street Mill with its clattering looms. They will meet Conrad Varley who is a cotton weaving man to his fingertips and had his own mill until the late 1970s.'

Opposite the Helmshore complex is the Musbury Mill retail outlet which is run by Adrian Mitchell, who has long and fond connections with the mill:

'My family have been cotton folk for three generations and this mill is in my blood. Musbury was a deer park in medieval times and the mill building I now own has hardly changed at all since 1890. Where we now sell fabric was once a spinning floor and the bosses went to Manchester to buy raw cotton and also to sell on our finished product. The railway line is now closed and is a sort of unofficial nature reserve but the station was once only a few yards

Adrian Mitchell has been fascinated by the history of his mill.

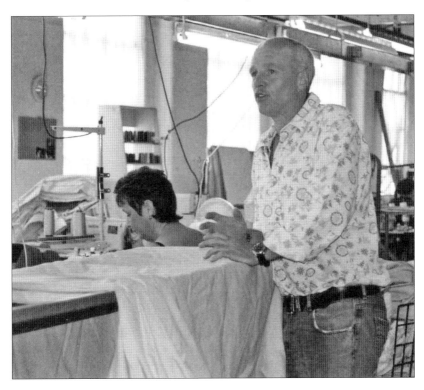

from the mill. From Helmshore the track went through Rawtenstall and on to Bury and Manchester. I like to sit on the nearby steam train now run by the East Lancashire Railway and think about those men of cotton. Things have to change but at least we are still in textiles and this old mill, like the words of the song, just "keeps rolling along". I still work hard and I also play hard and enjoy my holidays. Perhaps the Wakes weeks have gone but I will play my part in preserving our proud history. Finding the history of machines is easy and has been done before. I think what you have to do now that cotton has all but gone in Lancashire is to set down the memories of folk who worked in the mills spinning, weaving and finishing and preserve them for ever after.'

I suppose that the decision to abandon the Wakes holidays marks the end of the cotton empire in Lancashire. The next thing to disappear could be the language associated with the mills. I hope that these memories will help preserve the linguistic heritage of a county which prospered during the age of the three Cs – coal, canals and cotton! Many of the words still in use today relate to the history of cotton and a dictionary of these terms is the subject of the chapter which follows.

Chapter 6

The Language of Cotton

Lancashire, like all counties, has its own words and dialects which need some translation to enable 'off cumdens' to understand them, as I discovered whilst writing *Lankie Twang*. In the case of the cotton, or more accurately, the textile industry there is what can be described as a language within a language. As time goes by and more and more mills have closed the words and phrases evolved therein have remained. This glossary explains some of the words which have been spun and woven into everyday speech and writing.

Alley In the 1930s Gracie Fields sang a hit song about 'Sally in our Alley' but what technically speaking was an alley? Was it a back street in her tome town of Rochdale? Possibly, but it is just as likely to have described the narrow space between the spinning frames and noisy weaving looms. It is thought that most of the steps used by Lancashire clog dancers were devised to fit in to these narrow alleys and the rhythm of the tunes replicated the sound of the machinery.

The Ossie Cloggers outside Accrington Town Hall – they have performed throughout Europe and the United States.

Asshole This is not an insult but a corruption of 'ash hole'. This was the space between the coal-fired mill boilers, the fires of which had to be regularly raked out and re-stoked. The men operating them needed great physical strength as well as the skill to maintain the correct temperature and pressure. A few men still do this and can be seen hard at work in places such as Queen Street Mill Museum in Burnley, the Ellenroad Engine House at Milnrow and at Bancroft Mill in Barnoldswick.

Back to back When we speak of 'back to back' victories in sport we do not appreciate that there is a textile connection. Houses for mill workers were initially built as cheaply as possible and two dwellings shared a back wall, so that each had a front door but no rear entrance. Some of these houses still exist and many are now much sought after. There is a fine example around the Pasture Lane area of Barrowford, near Nelson.

Baggin Until canteens were provided for the workers from the 1950s onwards, meals often had to be eaten standing up in the gaps between the machines. Workers on piece work often preferred to keep working whilst eating their 'baggin'. Rose Chamberlain of Darwen recalls: 'Afore we had a proper canteen we et our baggin in t'alley. My mother and me lived next door to t'boilerman and he would sometimes let us warm up our food and tea close to his fire.'

Bant The word referred to a cloth of poor quality and until fairly recently in some districts an unruly or untidy child was referred to as a bantling.

Batterer This did not refer to one who ill-treated his wife and children or a successful boxer but a strong man who could physically beat raw cotton into workable fibres. In the early days there were lots of batterers and the name remained long after machines took over this essential process.

Beamer Cricket commentators refer to this and umpires frown upon bowlers who deliver the leather at the head of a batsman. Lancashire cotton workers, however, have an entirely different explanation of the word, as Rene Donley of Burnley told me: 'Beamers were people who wound the warp from the bobbins of cotton and fixed them onto the beam of the loom. The beam was a heavy lump of polished wood. The man then had literally to lift his beam onto the loom and everybody could then "get weaving".'

Billy A device for reducing the long cotton threads (called the slub) and twisting them ready to be placed on the spinning frame.

Bobbin We are all accustomed to seeing a bobbin of cotton in our homes but those in cotton mills were very large. In the days of cotton, bobbin mills were essential as I found when I spoke to Mike Neild who works at the Stott Park bobbin mill near Lakeside in Cumbria, who told me, 'English Heritage has restored

Bobbin winding in a spinning mill.

our mill to full working order and it looks much as it did when cotton was important. We even have the old water-wheel and the steam engine which replaced it and both are in full working order.' I have fond memories of this place in the 1940s when I went in the school holidays to deliver their baggin to the fathers of a couple of my classmates. Until the 1950s bobbin mills were found all over northern England, many situated close to the managed woodlands which provided the raw materials.

Box Harry Week Jane Horrocks, who worked as a weaver in Rossendale for 30 years starting in 1942, told me: 'One expression which is dying out these days is what my mother who was also a weaver called Box Harry Week. This meant that folk were often hard up as the next pay day approached. We had our money separated into boxes to cover things like rent, coal and insurance but we also had one in reserve which we called Box Harry. If an emergency arose Harry was raided.'

Bullocking This was not a rude word but a time at the end of the working day in the mill. Joyce Milner pointed out: 'We each had to clean our own machinery and were not paid for it which meant nobody liked having to do the bullocking. When we went onto shift work we had to clean our looms for the weaver on the next shift. There were many rows when one weaver found that the last worker had not done a proper bullocking.'

Butty Although this word now has a general usage there is a firm cotton connection. During a brief conversation with Gracie Fields on the island of Capri I heard the word used in the proper context. She overheard me with my northern accent saying to my companion that I was off for a cup of coffee and she quipped, 'Good for you, lad. Off tha goes to t'butty shop.' Many of the early mill owners had food or butty shops attached to their workplace and often forced workers to buy from these. The products were often of very inferior quality, with some of the wheat in the bread substituted with oat meal or even sawdust! The only fillings which most folk could afford were either beef dripping or treacle. The prices at the 'butty shops' were high and soon workers were objecting to being cheated. At Rochdale in the 1840s a group of workers set up their own co-operative store and from this humble beginning the Co-operative Society began. All this fascinating history, which began with cotton operatives, is graphically explained in the Co-op Museum on Toad Lane in Rochdale. Periodically the money spent at the Co-op was added up and a rebate was given to each shopper and this windfall was abbreviated from dividend to 'divi'.

Caddon A cover of thick unbleached cotton or other fabric.

Calico This is a cotton cloth but with patterns woven into it. The name derives from 'Calicut', a port on the west coast of Malabar to the south of old Madras.

Chit A chitty was the name of a young girl, often under ten, who worked with a weaver and who was usually a female relative. This chit of a girl kept the loom free of loose fibres and provided any other assistance needed. This 'mere chit' eventually became a weaver in her own right after being trained at her mother's apron strings.

Copster Another name for a spinner and derived from cob or cop as in a spider's cobweb. Copster Green is a hamlet between Blackburn, Wilpshire and Ribchester. In the early days of the Industrial Revolution spinning machines were located there.

Cotton Men A group term for those who travelled by rail from the Lancashire towns to the Manchester Cotton Exchange to buy and sell textiles.

Counts A measure of the fineness of a yarn. Initially the calculation revealed the number of threads in a length measuring 840 yards. It also reflected the number of hanks which weighed one pound. The higher the count the thinner and finer the cloth would be and a consistency of count was essential. Cotton men always carried in their pocket a magnifying glass called a 'counting glass'. They could therefore predict the quality of their finished product by knowing the thread count.

Croft This common surname has its origins in the early days of the textile industry. A croft was a large area where the cloth (initially wool or linen) was pegged out during the long period of bleaching. The time taken for this was very dependent on the weather and many people short of ready cash watched anxiously as they viewed the progress. The piece of fabric was kept clear of the ground by a frame with hooks on it. These were called 'tenter hooks' and we still wait on 'tenterhooks' as we anticipate the completion of a task or for an event to start.

Dandy Those asked to list their favourite childhood comics might include the *Dandy*, but not many would know the origin of the word in the Lancashire textile context. The dandy was a small handloom capable of weaving very fine cloth which commanded a high price. Weavers skilled in the operation of these machines made a good living. They were often very arrogant and wore expensive clothes, including a top hat with a £5 note in the band. These men were called 'dandies' and in Blackburn they would parade around an area which became known as the 'dandy walk'. When the Americans refer to 'feeling fine and dandy', they are harking back to the textile trade.

Doffer A vital job in a spinning mill. A person who changed the spools on a mule without stopping the machine. Doreen Howard worked in a Bury mill: 'It was hard graft. I started off doffing when I was 14 and then I were a weaver at Joshua Hoyles Mill in Summerseat near Ramsbottom. This mill overlooks the river Irwell and it is now converted into posh flats

A doffer at work in the Pilot Mill on Alfred Street in Bury. Taken in 1950, this shows a friend of Bessie Johnson who worked hard to achieve equal pay for women in the mills. She died in 2006 at the age of 95.

called Spinning Apartments. Grafting Apartments would have been a better name.'

Doggers out Up until the Second World War great efforts were made in Lancashire (and probably elsewhere) to stamp out 'illegal' gambling. Men would gather in remote places on the hills and play pitch and toss, which meant tossing coins with the one calling the correct side picking up the loot. To avoid the law, look-outs were posted and these were called 'doggers out'. A children's game was a variant of this and incorporated into a sort of hide and seek. In my village we called the game 'Ooh Dogs'.

Dresser In the cotton context this does not apply to a snappy dresser or an item of furniture but to the early days of weaving. Patterns were difficult to incorporate into the fabric but eventually intelligent and resourceful workers solved the problems. 'Warp dressers' were real craftsmen employed in mills. They specialised in weaving relatively short lengths with exclusive designs, which commanded high prices. They were the equivalent to modern day IT designers working on computers.

Fettling A term of affection in Lancashire is to greet a friend, 'Ow do, owd fettler!' I am surprised that there does not seem to be a surname of Fettler but it was a term used by the tacklers as they mended broken down machinery. As late as 2006 I overheard a conversation on a train from Blackburn to Manchester. A girl remarked to a friend, 'Aye, he's reet grand is mi dad. He can fettle owt.'

Goin' threw t'mill Even the boss's son had to start by doing the menial jobs and once he knew the ropes he could move up. A successful man in those days had literally 'gone through the mill'.

A warp dresser at work.

Heald This is a common surname in textile territory. The heald was the part of a loom on which the warp could be raised or lowered. The spaces between the healds were known as the threads.

Jacquard A variant of a loom which allows cloth to be woven into patterns. It was a very simple type of 'computer' which used punched cards set above the loom to allow several colours to be combined to produce often complex patterns.

Jean A thick hard-wearing cotton fustian. These days everyone has heard of jeans.

Jinny This is a variation on the Christian name Jenny but it actually means a machine. Hargreaves' spinning jenny may therefore have been his 'spinning Jenny'. Jinny Lane situated close to Pendle Hill between the villages of Roughlee and Newchurch may well mean an area where early spinning machines were in use.

Keep the band in the nick Some think that this phrase relates to the placing of a needle into the grooves of an old 78 rpm gramophone record. Actually it dates back much further to the days of mule spinning or bobbin winding. A string or band ran in a groove of a spinning device and when kept in motion kept the wheel rotating.

Kissing the shuttle Pat Whiteley showed me a shuttle and demonstrated how and why it was kissed: 'The best way to explain this is to look at the eye of the shuttle and try to thread the cotton through it. The best way to draw it through was to do it by sucking. This tasted unpleasant and because of the oil and other chemicals many weavers were made ill and I'm told that this is why the Christies cancer hospital was founded.'

Knocker up In the days before everyone had clocks, workers had to set off to the mill sometimes even before dawn. Each area had a knocker up who had usually retired from the mill and earned a

Pat Whiteley demonstrating the technique of kissing the shuttle.

few pennies from each worker by waking them up. The owd chap carried a long stick with a tuft of metal rods at the top. These rods were scraped on the bedroom window and he continued until the occupant of the bedroom responded. In 1958, when I was invited to stay at my girlfriend's (now my wife) house, her father pointed out the scratch marks made by the knocker up. This was in Newman Street, Burnley and when my in-laws died in the 1980s the marks were still visible.

A Burnley knocker up at work.

Lap 'Clean' cotton fibres which emerge from the carding engine. Aprons cut from the unwanted ends of cloth were called laps and were worn by mill workers to protect their clothing from oil.

Lappets Inexpensive striped cotton fabric particularly produced in the 19th century for Asian and Middle Eastern markets.

Limegal A breed of pony originating from Galloway in Scotland, sure-footed beasts used on the packhorse routes prior to the Industrial Revolution. Among the heavy loads carried were wool and cotton.

Lint Loose pieces of cotton accumulating around machinery, which had to be constantly swept clean.

Mash To Lancastrians this does not just refer to squashed potatoes but was also used to describe a badly produced piece of fabric which had to be rejected.

Mee-Maw This was the language of the weaving mill and was not spoken but mimed. There was no point in trying to speak in the noise and so lip reading became vital. Woe betide people in public places who insult an old weaver thinking she would never hear owt. Emma Brown told me: 'My husband and I were running a social at our local church playing a game called "Chinese market" in which one player had to mime an object and the others guess what it was. No spoken word was allowed. One group of ladies did very well and won hands down and as they were rather elderly I expressed surprise. My husband said it was easy because they were all weavers and they didn't need to speak it was all done by lip reading and signs.'

Old horse The Burnley weaver Marie Sagar told me in 2007 about 'the old horse' which stalked the local mills: 'All weavers worked on piece work and if there was a week when things went wrong and they did not earn much they used the "old horse". This meant that they fiddled their returns and then worked harder the following week to restore the balance. In some cases a weaver built up a backlog and if she was popular the others joined in to help and med sure that her old horse recovered.'

Overlooker Mrs Shirley Bellshaw of Roughlee remembers the work of the overlooker: 'As weavers we knew that the overlookers were hawk-eyed folk whose job it was to check the quality of the cloth which came off our looms. Rejected cloth meant a loss in wages and regular sub-standard work meant the sack. We were terrified of a visit from the overlooker.'

Picker A piece of leather which hits the shuttle and bounces it across the loom. The used pickers were often taken home for the pet dogs to chew, they were excellent for their teeth and the oil helped their coats to shine.

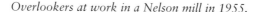

Overlookers at work in a Nelson mill in 1955.

Picking The process of sending the shuttle through the space between the warp threads.

Piece A length of cloth on which pay rates were calculated. A typical cotton piece measured 28 yards.

Piecer A worker, paid on piece rates, who tied together the broken ends of yarn on a spinning mule. On huge moving machines this required nimble fingers and quick feet. Piecers and the children who helped them (little piecers) worked barefoot.

Playing Mill workers' term for being out of work. Also known as 'laiking'.

Plug Drawing Refers to the riots of 1830-1840 when new steam-operated machines were being wrecked. One way was to knock the plugs out of the boilers which at best would stop work but often caused explosions.

Pop shop The name for a pawn shop, as in 'pop goes the weasel'.

Popping your clogs The death of a cotton worker, who no longer needed their clogs.

Poverty knock A period between 1830 and the 1850s when handloom weaving was replaced by power looms. The traditional knocking sounds of the handloom fell silent. The 'poverty knock' was used to describe this silence. Also adapted for the sound of those demanding outstanding rent or other unpaid bills.

Purring This has nowt to do with your pet moggy but was a vicious game which often resulted in very serious injuries. Contests involved prize money and there was lots of betting on the results. Two lusty lads wearing clogs with their irons sharpened held each other around the neck and kicked each other until one gave way. Massive cuts, bruises and broken bones were usual and teachers had their work cut out to stop young boys learning to purr in preparation for future lucrative victories.

Putter out This is not a modern term for a night club bouncer but a vital part of the cotton industry. Any person with a modest surplus of cash could buy first wool and, later, cotton in bulk. All that he then had to do was to travel around the countryside supplying the raw material which local people would process for him. The textile historian, Joan Evans told me:

'The putter out must have been busy, travelling to Liverpool to buy raw cotton and then selling the goods finished by the people who came to him to receive cotton goods for processing.'

Marlene Jaques takes up the story:

'In the 1970s I was the personal assistant to the Managing Director of the Reeves Brothers Mill in Padiham. They made hospital clothing and shrouds and had lots of workers inside the mill but there was a greater volume of work which could not be processed in the mill itself. We therefore employed lots of out-workers who were provided with machines in their own homes and processed the items on piece rates. This putting out system has therefore continued right up to the present time but obviously on a much reduced scale.'

Reacher in An assistant to a power loom weaver who literally reached into a machine and corrected any minor malfunction.

Reed A metal comb-like structure on a loom which determined how fine the finished cloth would be. The reed also guided the shuttle to ensure that the weave remained tight.

Reel A revolving machine on which the yarn was wound into yanks.

Ring Frame A spinning machine where each spindle revolved inside a ring. Friction and space was therefore reduced to a minimum.

Roving Frame A machine to strengthen the twist of the cotton fibres. These strengthened rovings were then ready for a finished yarn to be guaranteed with regard to the customer's specification.

Scrutching, slubbing and steaming These terms bear no relation to any form of ablution. Scrutching was beating raw bolls of cotton and then separating out any unwanted debris from the fibres. This waste debris was often referred to as trash. Slubbing is a method of arranging slivers of cotton onto a machine called a drawing frame. This literally drew all the twisted threads straight. Steaming was creating the humid conditions essential for the efficient working of cotton; this created an atmosphere which was most unhealthy for those who worked in the mills.

Sparkies A game played by youngsters scraping the irons of their clogs on the flagstones and making sparks.

Tackling The tacklers in mills were the men who repaired the looms and kept them running. Weavers were often annoyed when they thought that a tackler was either lazy, inefficient or both.

Twister This is not an insulting word for an untrustworthy person but a term used in the textile trade from at least 1579. It refers to a worker who spins thread and then twists together the yarn of a new

Conrad Varley demonstrates the work of a twister at Queen Street Mill, Burnley.

warp with an existing one. Also known as 'twirlers', they did not become redundant when machines were produced to tie the knots, but a wary eye had to be kept when a thread snapped. I always envied my late father-in-law, Wilf Jaques who could tie knots using one hand and could do this with either his left or right hand. I watched him by his Barber and Coleman twisting machine, reacting to any break with great speed and skill.

Warp Threads which run lengthways across the loom. Warping was the process of winding the warp onto the beam of a loom, which at times could be physically very demanding.

Weft Thread which runs crossways on the loom.

Yarn A technical term for a spun thread.

Chapter 7

The Last Rites: A Sad Cotton Wake

In 1914, 40% of the textiles in the world came from Lancashire, and Oldham had more spinning spindles than the whole of France and Germany put together – 600,000 people were involved in spinning and above 85% of cotton cloth was exported. Lancashire's only worry was whether it could find sufficient supplies of raw cotton.

After the First World War there was a boom period as Europe, the Commonwealth and the USA demanded more and more fabric. This did not last long and many Lancashire firms suffered by being too much in search of quick profits and reluctant to invest in new machines.

By the 1920s a decline had set in from which the industry would never recover. The people who worked in cotton, however, were still euphoric at the end of the conflict of the First World War and ready to roll up their sleeves and return to peacetime work. Pat Young, who now lives near Balderstone, told me that the Preston Guild of 1922 had a cotton theme to it.

In 1912, 8,000 million miles of cloth had been produced, but by

1922 GUILD. PRESTON. ARCH of COTTON BALES. No 15.

A very rare postcard showing cotton as a main theme during the Preston Guild of 1922.

the 1930s 4,000 miles was regarded as a record and it was exports which had suffered most. This slack period is still remembered by many who lived in the cotton belt during the hungry thirties. Unemployment was only reduced during the Second World War as cotton mills diversified.

Joyce Kilshaw, who worked as a weaver in Darwen, knew that India Mill relied on exports to the sub-continent:

'I remember Percy Davies, who was a rich chap and an MP who was a strong socialist, showing Gandhi around the town on what they described as a fact finding mission. I remember his skeletal body and his long "dress" and we guessed what he was up to. He knew that it made economic sense to produce cloth in India rather than paying for material produced in Lancashire. This is what happened after Indian independence in 1947. We saw this as the start of a major decline in our industry.'

There was something of a false dawn after the war because even though other countries were setting up their own mills, they still needed the machines to put in them. Bob Kelly worked in an iron foundry in Burnley: 'We were kept busy in the 1950s meltin' down iron to be sent to places like Howard and Bullough in Accrington. They were making machines which were sent all round the world while my mates who worked in the mills were finding it hard to find jobs.'

In retrospect it has to be said that the mill owners did not appreciate the grave situation and refused to spend money on new and more efficient machines. They preferred to stick it out and hope that their smaller competitors would close down and thus capture their share of the market and also poach the best craftsmen and women. This certainly was the case with Wilfred Jaques, as his daughter Marlene remembers, in the 1950s and the early 1960s:

'My dad in a way was a victim of his skill. As the mills started closing down he was job poached and towards the end he worked in many mills helping them to keep going. He was pleased to stay in work but unfortunately he was moved on from one mill to another and missed out on redundancy.'

Alice Latimer also remembers the hard times in Bury:

'We could always tell when Dad was in or out of work. Good weeks we got three pennies spending money but when he was off work we only got one, but he usually made sure that it was a shiny new one.'

Obviously, when woven fabrics were not being sold this meant that the spinning mills also had little work. Some districts, however, were affected more than others. Oldham, for example, produced a coarse yarn and found the going tough whilst for those mills in Bolton which produced a finer yarn markets were easier to find.

From the 1950s cotton was coming under threat from two other sources which should have been but which were not anticipated. Firstly, large companies were moving in and buying up as many small family firms as possible, explaining that 'rationalisation' was the only way to compete in a world market. Secondly, man-made fibres were beginning to take the place of natural fibres and the rayon-based factories were assuming dominance. In 1937 less than 10% of fabric was rayon-based but by the late 1960s this situation had been largely reversed.

Eric Goddan of Brierfield remembers this period very well:

'One thing I will always remember are the family names of some of the cotton workers. As I talk to you I am thinking of Bracewell Spencer and Atkinson Broxup. Bracewell had a fierce bull terrier which would not let anybody in the house. I had the sad job of visiting his house after Bracewell died at work. The dog let us in as if it knew why we were there. I still find this sad and very creepy. I worked with so many great characters. In the course of my life in the mill I literally went "through the mill". I began as a weaver, then worked as a tackler and then in the office as a manager. I was able to look out on both sides of the fence and I could see the problems as cotton declined. As first one mill closed and then another, I had to move in search of work. By 1982, however, there was no work left for any on us and I had to retire. I loved the job and if there had been work to do I would have carried on till I snuft it.'

Another factor which has not often been brought to the fore has been a change in attitude following the end of the war. Neither the new Labour government nor, especially, the workers were prepared to allow the working conditions which once pertained in mills to continue. Many workers who had toiled in munitions factories for good wages did not want to return to the grind of the mill for much less pay.

This led to a shortage of labour in the cotton industry and this was solved by attracting migrant workers, especially those from the Indian sub-continent.

June Fielden, who worked as a weaver in this climate of change, remembers the contrast very well indeed:

'When I started work in t'mill in 1932 we had nowhere to eat our food properly and the place were damp. There were bits of cotton all ower t'spot but in 1950 they had cleaned the place up and we had a bit more space between t'looms. We had a canteen where we could sit and have a decent brew. One mill even had a room where babies could be looked after. In 1935 I had to beg for a job but by 1952 the mills were chasing weavers and t'boot were on t'other foot.'

The two mills in the Roe Lee area of Blackburn were anxious to attract more and more women weavers.

The weavers working in the two Roe Lee Mills in Blackburn. This dates to the 1940s when the decline of cotton had not quite set in.

It was easy during this period for those who lost their jobs to 'blame the bosses' but the smaller mill owners, and later all of the family firms, were being squeezed ever more tightly until all but a very few had to admit defeat and close down. Some companies were so desperate for orders that they purchased sales vans. Hawkins Cottons of Preston set up a number of these publicity vans in 1953, as mentioned in chapter 5. Although successful for a while the writing was not just on the vans but on the wall and the decline in orders was sadly terminal.

Other firms spent lots of money on colourful adverts; the Trutex Company published very attractive postcards to send to existing and potential clients. Huge firms such as Horrockses, Crewdson and Company, with bases in Preston, Manchester, Bolton and London, could fight off competition for longer than smaller competitors but still lost the final battle. They published many books on cotton and the life of John Horrocks, who founded his firm in 1791, has been chronicled several times.

Some firms were quite enlightened as they searched for the best workers. In the Horrockses' mills around the Preston area especially, first aid rooms, rest rooms and even good nurseries for young children were provided at the company's expense.

Some mill workers were sadly able to witness the last rites and when I spoke at some length to Pat Whiteley, who now lives near Clitheroe, she told me:

'I worked at the Roe Lee Mill in Blackburn and we were weaving a brocade with lovely patterns on it and which was used to make wedding dresses. When the mill closed it was sad because outstanding orders had to be fulfilled right up to the end. I was the very last weaver to shut down my looms and there were a tear in my eye because I were just one week short of working 24 years in this mill. They could weave this brocade much cheaper abroad and we could not compete with their prices.'

One factor which was perhaps just as important was that the

Spinning rooms, 1860 (above) and 1960 (below) – note only one operative is in view in 1960 and she is wearing high heels!

Lancashire mill owners either could not or would not invest in new technology. Keith Hall has one of the finest collections of textile-based postcards that I have ever seen. Keith pointed out to me,

'I have photographs of mills taken in 1860 and others dating to the mid 1960s and they don't look much different. It is only when you look at the clothes that the workers were wearing that you realise that these scenes were more than 100 years apart. There seems to have been little effort to install any sort of new technology.'

Many mill workers, some very skilled operatives, had to solve the problems associated with not having a job by emigrating. Others decided to stick it out and hope but most were like Roger Upton, who still works in and around mills and lives in Tottington near Bury:

'I looked after the heavy goods vehicles at Smethursts Bleachers and Dyers Mill at Woolfold in Bury. It was an old fashioned mill with its own engineering shop which was driven by belts from huge shafts powered by the Lancashire boilers. It even had a full joiners' workshop with lathes and saws etc on a mezzanine floor above the engineering shop. This was also powered by boilers. The workshop included a forge operated by Billy Platt, the blacksmith. Billy could make brackets and fittings for anything in the mill. He was also making wrought-iron gates and ornaments for just about everyone in the area. During the holiday shut-down maintenance was carried out all over the mill, this included having the flues cleaned on the boilers. This was a filthy job and the men emerging from the grates were black from head to toe. The boilers also acted as an unofficial crematorium for family pets in the area.'

Jim Brodie has memories of the shift of cotton from its dominance in Lancashire to other parts of the world:

'In 1957 I visited the Textile Machinery Manufacturers

Annual Exhibition held at Belle Vie in Manchester. We were feeling the pinch at the Casablanca's High Draft Company and the firm brought its exhibit in lorry number 16. Actually we only had one but the number gave the impression of having a whole fleet! The exhibition attracted visitors from all over the world including Japanese armed with batteries of cameras. Most countries bought one of our machines but then learned how to copy them and we were soon suffering from lack of orders. Speaking to other companies it became obvious that our days of good business were over for good.'

Before blaming the mill owners for all the ills of the cotton industry it was important for me to speak to those men who had to close down mills which had been in their families for as many as four generations.

Even staunch trade unionists like Rex Gormley realised that there were additional factors to consider:

'It had been easy to blame the conflict and greed of unions and owners for the decline but it was not true then and it is certainly not true now. As a worker, a unionist and a man who worked in the office, we could all see what was happening and could do nowt about it. If anybody was to blame it was the government who interfered without understanding the industry itself. Even this would not have helped in the long run because international companies with money and world markets moved in. They first squeezed small mills and then bought them out. They ran them until all their reserve raw materials were done and then closed them. They then stripped the machinery and shipped it abroad to be reassembled where labour costs were minimal as food were cheaper there. They then sold the shell of the mill and went on to their next victim. These factors could clearly be seen by all of us and we felt so bloody helpless.'

A reminder of a bygone age – Hesketh and Sons' spinning mill in Bolton.

The last word, however, should be from Peter Hargreaves:

'It is sad to think that although many of us fought tooth and nail to keep Lancashire cotton on the world map there were so many factors stacked against us and we lost the battle. My family are still determined to market textiles but geography, world markets and economics, especially cheap labour abroad, made it impossible to do it all within the county we love. We must, however, never forget that Lancashire gave to the world the textile technology and thankfully this expertise looks likely to continue for some time yet. The memories of those who owned, ran and worked in our mills should be a testimony to the age when

*The last rites of the old shuttle looms in the early 1990s.
This is Moor Mill in 1991.*

cotton was indeed king. We have retained the marketing and sales operation within our historic buildings.'

Lancashire's proud history and traditions should be celebrated, as should the people who helped to write of these events.

Further Reading

Aspin C. and Chapman S. F., *James Hargreaves and the Spinning Jenny* (Helmshore Local History Society, 1964)

Bullen A. and Fowler D., *The Cardroom Workers Union* (Union Publication, 1986)

Burton A., *The Rise and Fall of King Cotton* (Deutsch and BBC, 1984)

Chapman S.D., *The Cotton Industry in the Industrial Revolution* (Macmillan, 1972)

Clark H., *Textile Printing* (Shire, 1997)

Freethy R., *Lankie Twang* (Countryside Books, 2004)

Freethy R., *Lancashire 1939-1945 Working for Victory* (Countryside Books, 2007)

Hopwood E., *The Lancashire Weavers' Story* (Amalgamated Weavers' Association, 1971)

Longmate N., *The Hungry Mills* (Temple Smith, 1978)

Peroni R., *Industrial Lancashire in Photographs* (Hendon Publishing, 1976)

Rose M.B. (ed), *The Lancashire Cotton Story* (Lancashire County Books, 1996)

Sandberg L.G., *Lancashire in Decline* (Ohio State University, 1993)

Sandiford A.V. and Ashworth T.E., *The Forgotten Valley* (Bury and District History Society, 1981)

Singleton J., *Lancashire on the Scrapheap* (Oxford University Press, 1991)

Tippet L.H.C., *A Portrait of the Lancashire Textile Industry* (Oxford University Press, 1969)

Wood and Wilmore, *The Romance of the Cotton Industry* (Oxford University Press, 1927)

Index